Herschel Island

Yukon River   Fort Yukon   Rampart House
Porcupine River   La Pierre's House

Peace River

Selkirk

Mackenzie River

Kilkerran
Pouce Coupe

Whitehorse   Fort Wrigley
Carcross
Bennet City   Tagish Lake   Fort Simpson
Skagway   Atlin

Fort Liard

Chilco

Telegraph Creek   Tahl Tan
Glenora

Stikine River

Fort George

CALEDONIA

Antler Creek

Peace River Block

Quesnel   Barkerville
Mosquito Creek
Antler
Keithley

Williams Lake   150 Mile House

NEW WESTMINSTER

CARIBOO

B.C.

KOOTENAY

Fraser River

Columbia River

Clinton

Donald
Golden

Pavilion
Ashcroft   Thompson River
Lillooet
Creekside
Kamloops

Revelstoke

Arrowhead

Lake

Lytton   Nicomen
Shulus   Nicola
Vernon

Windermere

Port Douglas
Boston Bar
Spuzzum
Westbank

Lardeau
Kaslo

Kootenay Lake

Kootenay River

Harrison Lake
Yale
Emory's Bar
Hope

aple Ridge
mond
Chilliwack
Langley

Penticton

Nelson

Fort Steele

Fernie

Keremeos
Fairview

Cranbrook
Wild Horse Creek
Moyie

Osoyoos   Phoenix   Rossland   Trail
Grand Forks

# THE ANGLICAN CHURCH IN BRITISH COLUMBIA

1959

*The*

# ANGLICAN CHURCH
## *in British Columbia*

FRANK A. PEAKE, *M.A., B.D.*

MITCHELL PRESS   *Vancouver, B.C.*

The text of this book is set in 12 point
Eldorado and the chapter headings are
24 point Garamond. Two thousand five
hundred copies of this first edition have
been printed and bound at Vancouver,
Canada, by Mitchell Press Limited.

March, 1959

PRINTED IN CANADA

# Table of Contents

# Illustrations

# Abbreviations

C.M.S.    *Church Missionary Society*

C. & C.C.S.    *Colonial and Continental Church Society—*
*now, Colonial and Commonwealth Church Society*

B.C. & Y.C.A.S.    *British Columbia and Yukon Church Aid Society*
*(formerly British Columbia Church Aid Society)*

S.P.C.K.    *Society for the Promotion of Christian Knowledge*

S.P.G.    *Society for the Propagation of the Gospel*

M.S.C.C.    *Missionary Society of the Church in Canada*

# Foreword

*By The Archbishop of British Columbia*

THE centenary of British Columbia in 1958 has brought
a great revival of interest in the history of our Province and its
institutions, and not least in the story of its religious life. The first
regular Anglican services on the Pacific slope began in 1837, and
in 1859 the Diocese of British Columbia was established with
Dr. George Hills as the first bishop. Since then the diocese has
been divided several times. This book may be regarded as part
of the hundredth anniversary of the first bishop's consecration,
wherein we give thanks to Almighty God for all that He has
done to prosper the brave pioneer work of Bishop Hills and his
band of devoted associates. We may truly say that Hills planted,
Sillitoe, Ridley, Good, Collison and countless others watered,
but God gave the increase.

The author of this book, Professor Frank A. Peake, is the
Archivist of the Ecclesiastical Province, and, in commending his
work to the clergy and laity, I am happy to express my grateful
appreciation of the research and study which he has so cheerfully
and effectively undertaken in the interests of the Church in this
Province.

*Harold Columbia*

Bishop's Close,
Victoria.

# Introduction

THIS BOOK has been prompted by a growing interest on my part in the life and work of the Church in western Canada, and by the realisation that although there is a wealth of material dealing with particular regions there is no book which tells the story of Anglicanism in British Columbia and the Yukon as a whole. By its nature the book is necessarily selective and makes no attempt to discuss all the details of our corporate life. Not everyone will agree with the selection made but I have tried to trace in broad outline the development of the Church in what is now the Ecclesiastical Province of British Columbia. It is essentially a book of beginnings and some will be disappointed by the arbitrary terminal dates which have been used. Originally it had been my intention to use the outbreak of the First World War as a convenient *terminus ad quem* but there have been many significant "beginnings" since then, as, for example, the establishment of the Provincial Synod, the formation of the Diocese of Cariboo, and the opening of the Provincial Theological College in its present home on the grounds of the University of

British Columbia. Generally speaking, the closing date of this history is about 1927.

It is a joy to acknowledge the help and co-operation afforded me in many quarters: from the Archbishop and bishops of the Province who have enabled me to have free access to synod documents; to Willard E. Ireland, the Provincial Archivist, and Miss Inez Mitchell, his assistant, for unfailing help at the Provincial Archives, Victoria; to the students in my Church History seminars for their questions and general interest, and to Edward S. Gale, also a student of the Anglican Theological College, who has been of invaluable service in preparing the index and making drawings for the end-papers.

*F. A. Peake*

The Anglican Theological College,
Vancouver, B.C.

# THE ANGLICAN CHURCH IN BRITISH COLUMBIA

# The Honourable
# Company and its
# Chaplains

SIR, if you wish to know why a cow's tail grows downward,
I cannot tell you. I can only cite the fact." Such was the reply
said to have been made by a frustrated chaplain at Fort Vancouver to the Hudson's Bay Company resident chief factor who had
just demanded an explanation of the strictures on his administration contained in the chaplain's report.

But for the beginning of the story we must go back to the visit
to the Columbia in 1824-1825 of George Simpson, newly
appointed Governor of the Hudson's Bay Company after its
1821 union with the North West Company. On the occasion
of his visit Simpson had written to the Governor and Committee
in London, "I do not know any part of North America where
the natives could be civilized and instructed in morality and
religion at such a moderate expense and with so much facility as
on the Banks of the Columbia River. . . . The praiseworthy zeal
of the Missionary Society in the cause of Religion I think would

here be soon crowned with success. . . ."[1] At the same time he was careful to add that the missionary sent "ought to be cool and temperate in his habits and of a Mild conciliatory disposition even tempered and not too much disposed to find fault with any little laxity of Morals he may discover at the Company's Establishment. . . ."[2] Particularly, said Simpson, should he be tolerant of the fact that many of the gentlemen and employees of the Company had contracted "fur trade marriages," unions which though permanent had received neither the blessing of the Church nor the sanction of the State. In 1830 the Governor and Committee in London informed Simpson that a clergyman was to be sent out "as a missionary for the West Side of the Mountains"[3] but no missionary arrived.

Six years later, in August, 1836, the promised missionary appeared in the person of the Reverend Herbert Beaver, B.A. (Cantab.) who was to be both chaplain and schoolmaster. Beaver was not the clergyman Simpson had envisaged. He "was a man below the medium height, light brown hair, gray eyes, light complexion, a feminine voice, with large pretensions to oratory, a poor delivery, and no energy. His ideas of clerical dignity were such, that he felt himself defiled and polluted in descending to 'the common herd of savages' he found on arriving at Vancouver. The governor was uncivil, the clerks were boors, the women were savages. There was not an individual about the establishment he felt he could associate with.'"[4] Although the faults were not all on Beaver's side it is apparent that he was hardly a fit candidate for the post he had come to fill.

There had been a school in operation at Fort Vancouver since 1832, when it had been started at Dr. John McLoughlin's invitation by John Ball, a New England teacher and lawyer turned trader who found himself in Oregon that winter without employment and without means. When Beaver arrived, McLoughlin, the Chief Factor, turned the school over to him, and the missionary reported it as

> consisting of about sixty scholars, one third being Girls, of various ages, from five to fourteen years, which having been under different teachers for some time past, had lately been placed under the management of Mr. John Fisher Robinson. The first and second Classes, amounting to fourteen, read well, write tolerably, and begin to cypher, but have received little religious education, the singing of hymns, as I understand, forming nearly the whole. The other Classes are in different Stages of progress. To this school I was in the habit of devoting much daily attention, and Mrs. Beaver received the girls in her own apartment every morning from nine till twelve, except Saturdays and Sundays, the former being a holiday, and on the latter day I was accustomed to catechise both sexes together.[5]

Beaver also hoped to provide instruction for the children of surrounding Indian tribes but felt this would need to wait until he had mastered Chinook jargon which served as a *lingua franca* for the coastal Indians.

In handing the school over to the new chaplain, McLoughlin gave strict instructions that the religious training of the Roman Catholic children was not to be interfered with, and saw that a list of pupils indicating their religious affiliations was supplied. Of this list, Beaver wrote:

> On inspecting this list I discovered that the C's [Roman Catholics] vastly to predominate, in fact, with but few exceptions, to the names of all the children, who were not too young to derive much benefit from the services of a clergyman; and seeing that mine, if this state of things were allowed to continue, were well nigh useless in the school, I set myself to analyze the pretensions of each child to be educated as a Protestant, or as a Roman Catholic; when, I found that there were only three or four who could with the least shadow of propriety be classed as the latter. The others, to whose names the Catholic mark had been affixed, were to be brought up in that faith for the most frivolous reasons. . . .[6]

3

Here is one of the first indications of Beaver's unwillingness to accept conditions as he found them. Mrs. Narcissa Whitman, the wife of the Presbyterian missionary who had just arrived, and who was scarcely likely to be prejudiced in favour of the Roman Catholics, said of the school that "it consists of about fifty-one children who have French fathers and Indian mothers. All the labourers here are Canadian French, with Indian wives. Indeed, some of the gentlemen of the Company have native wives. . . . French is the prevailing language spoken here. English is spoken only by a few." [7]

Beaver, however, was not prepared to face the facts and felt the Chief Factor's advice and instruction to be an impertinent interference with his perogatives. Later in the year McLoughlin withdrew the charge of the school from Beaver and wrote to the Governor and Committee in London expressing his dissatisfaction with their appointee. He then added insult to injury by inviting two Congregationalist ladies to look after it! There were, in all probability, Mrs. Narcissa Whitman and Mrs. Henry Spalding.

Beaver replied by writing to the women forbidding them to interfere in a matter which he considered his exclusive preserve. This letter came into the hands of the Chief Factor who wrote to Beaver describing it as an insult to the Company and demanding an explanation. Beaver denied the insult and claimed that he was responsible only to the Governor and Committee in London from whom he held his appointment. Moreover, Beaver had taken it upon himself to write to England criticizing Company policy on the Columbia. Strife between the two men increased until finally they came to blows. The occasion was given by one of Beaver's reports. Naturally McLoughlin read the reports before they were despatched but for a time he did no more than fume inwardly at their criticisms. Eventually, his patience exhausted and after reading one such report, he happened to meet the chaplain in the fort yard. Shaking the offending document, and in a voice which could be heard throughout the settlement, the Chief Factor demanded an explanation. This occasioned Beaver's classic reply, "Sir, if you wish to know why a cow's tail grows downward, I cannot tell you; I can only cite the fact." McLoughlin's fury knew no bounds. Without pausing to reflect he brought his cane down upon the shoulders of the self-righteous cleric.[8] The next day the Chief Factor apologized publicly for his conduct but Beaver refused to accept the apology and the tension grew.

It is almost certain that Beaver would have returned to England within months of his arrival had he not been petitioned to remain by a number of the residents, including a fair proportion of the Roman Catholics.[9] Although Beaver remained he had no hand in the school while McLoughlin was present but in March, 1838, the Chief Factor left on furlough. James Douglas, who now took charge of the fort, seems to have been kindly disposed towards the chaplain and actually allowed him to solemnize his fur trade marriage. Douglas encouraged Beaver in his work and returned the charge of the school to him, so that all seemed to be going well. In a despatch to the Governor and Committee, dated October 18th, 1838, but apparently drafted long before that date, Douglas said of the chaplain:

> The Church and School have been fully engaged in promoting moral and religious improvements, by diffusing the seeds of sound principles, and virtuous habits among the members of our little community, and to a portion of the Native population. . . . The attention of the Revd. Mr. Beaver to the duties of his office has been exemplary, and I think he has succeeded in awakening a more general desire for religious knowledge among the persons of his communion, than existed before his arrival.[10]

But before long, Beaver had also quarrelled with Douglas who felt it necessary to write a special letter to London explaining the circumstances. By this time it was quite apparent that Beaver could serve no useful purpose by remaining at Fort Vancouver and he and his wife returned to England. It is unfortunate that the first ventures in Anglican missions in the Pacific Northwest were obscured and hindered by a chaplain who, even in calmer and more settled circumstances, seems to have been a difficult and unco-operative soul.

Following the departure of the Beavers in November, 1838, the post of chaplain in the Columbia Department remained vacant for nearly ten years. During that time the headquarters of the Company were moved from Fort Vancouver on the Columbia to Fort Victoria at the southern tip of Vancouver Island. When Douglas went with his men to the new post on March 13th, 1843, he was accompanied by the Reverend Jean-Baptiste Bolduc, a Roman Catholic, who thus became the first missionary in the colony.

The next chaplain appointed by the Company was the Reverend Robert John Staines, B.A. (Cantab.), who proved to be scarcely less troublesome than his predecessor. He and his wife and nephew arrived at Victoria in the spring of 1849 and his function was to be primarily that of school-master. In fact, he was a layman at the time of his appointment but was told that if he took Holy Orders an additional £100 per annum would be allowed "for the performance of clerical duties as Chaplain to the Company."[11] His duties were not limited to those of a strictly clerical or education nature. Commander R. C. Mayne, in his book, *Four Years in British Columbia and Vancouver Island*, relates an amusing anecdote of the chaplain's experiences in connection with his care of the sick:

> The Indians are well known to be polygamists, but I believe that a plurality of wives is general only among the chiefs of tribes, the rest being commonly too poor to afford this luxury. No other cause for

any such abstinence on their part exists. When Mr. Stain[es] was the Colonial Chaplain at Victoria, the chief of the tribe residing there went to him for some medicine for his wife, who was ill. He gave him something which cured her, and, to the astonishment of the chaplain and his family, a day or two afterwards the chief came to his house, leading his wife by the hand, and, in gratitude for her recovery, presented her to his benefactor. On being remonstrated with, I believe, by the chaplain's wife, who objected, not at all unnaturally, to the nature of the offering, he said it was nothing, not worth mentioning in fact, as he could easily spare her, she being one of eleven.[12]

A school and residence for the Staines was to be built but at the time of their arrival nothing had been done and they were provided with accommodation in the fort which, by any standards, left much to be desired. A long description of the school has been preserved in the reminiscences of one of its pupils, Robert James Anderson, a son of Chief Factor A. C. Anderson. It would appear that Staines was of somewhat uncertain temper, a good teacher, "endowed with qualities calculated to win the respect and even love of those who were *en rapport* with him." At the same time, "Mrs. Staines was a much more energetic person, she it was who really kept the school going and in spite of many undoubtedly adverse circumstances managed comparatively most creditably."[13]

Douglas was well aware of the shortcomings of his schoolmaster but felt that on the whole his influence was beneficial, and expressed this in a letter to Chief Factor Anderson, of which the following is an excerpt:

The school is doing as well as can be expected in the circumstances. More assistance in the way of servants of respectable character is required than we have at our command; so many children give a great deal of trouble and I often wonder how Mrs. Staines can stand the fag of looking after them. She is invaluable and receives less assistance than she ought from her husband, who is rather lazy at times.

The children have greatly improved in their personal appearance

7

and one thing I particularly love in Staines is the attention he bestows on their religious training. Had I a selection to make he is not exactly the man I would choose; but it must be admitted we might find a man worse qualified for the charge of the school.[14]

Before long, however, Staines fell out with the Company officials; not on school matters but in connection with church affairs and the general policy of administration. As a result of Staines' activities in matters which were not his primary concern the school declined and by 1853 Douglas wrote to the Governor and Committee of the dissatisfaction among the parents of the pupils. In part, he said:

> I have . . . had a great deal of trouble in consequence of Mr. Staines' disagreeable manner, and unyielding temper, in keeping the school afloat, the subscribers being generally dissatisfied with his manage-ment, and had it not been for the interest expressed by the Governor and Committee in the success of the institution, I would have fol-lowed their example and closed my connection with it. As it is, Mr. Staines is an unsuccessful teacher, and the boys, who attend his school make so little progress, though Mrs. Staines is on the contrary more successful with the girls, that there nevertheless exists the utmost dissatisfaction among the subscribers with their general management; the school cannot therefore be much longer continued. . . .[15]

The officers in London could do nothing but throw the matter back to Douglas, intimating that he and his associates would be quite free to dispense with the services of Staines as schoolmaster but that it would be unwise to oust him from his post as chaplain at the same time and without adequate reason. Early in 1854 Staines was dismissed from the school. The story of his agitation against the Company's administration does not belong to an account of his work as chaplain and schoolmaster but it may suf-fice to say that he left the colony shortly after his dismissal from the school intending to return to England, but was drowned when the ship foundered off Cape Flattery.

8

There was one more chaplain of the Hudson's Bay Company on the "West Side of the Mountains" in the person of the Reverend Edward Cridge, but before we look at his long career in Victoria we must turn to other developments on the Pacific Coast.

---

1 Merk, Frederick, *Fur Trade and Empire*, Harvard University Press, Cambridge, 1931, p. 106.
2 *Ibid.*, p. 102.
3 *Ibid.*, p. 322.
4 Gray, W. H., *History of Oregon*, Harris & Holman, Portland, 1870, p. 162.
5 Jessett, Thomas E., "Herbert Beaver: First Anglican Clergyman West of the Rockies," *Historical Magazine of the Episcopal Church*, December, 1947, p. 419.
6 *Ibid.*, p. 420.
7 Eells, Myron, *Marcus Whitman, Pathfinder and Patriot*, The Alice Harriman Company, Seattle, 1909, p. 90.
8 Montgomery, Richard G., *The White-Headed Eagle*, Macmillan, New York, 1909, p. 239.
9 Jessett, op. cit., p. 424.
10 *Ibid.*, p. 427.
11 Slater, G. Hollis, "Rev. Robert Staines: Pioneer Priest, Pedagogue, and Political Agitator," *British Columbia Historical Quarterly*, October, 1950, p. 201.
12 Mayne, R. C., *Four Years in British Columbia and Vancouver Island*, John Murray, London, 1862, p. 276.
13 Slater, op. cit., p. 199.
14 Slater, op. cit., p. 201.
15 Slater, op. cit., p. 212.

# 2

# Early Missionary Ventures

REFERENCE has already been made to the removal of the western headquarters of the Hudson's Bay Company from the Columbia River to Vancouver Island. Something should now be said of the contemporary background. From the sixteenth century onwards the Pacific slope was a prize much sought after by the maritime trading powers of the day, a contest in which Britain, by sheer persistence, emerged as the survivor. After the American Revolution the new United States began to look casually westward and more particularly to the large area loosely described as the Oregon country. An agreement of joint occupancy, or more accurately, of equal rights, between Britain and the United States was signed in 1818 and renewed ten years later. By this agreement nationals of both countries were free to trade on the Pacific slope beyond the Rocky Mountains.

English trade in the region was exclusively in the hands of the Hudson's Bay Company whose chief factor, Dr. John Mc-

Loughlin, was appointed in 1824. During his twenty years in that capacity McLoughlin became almost a legend, maintaining peace with the Indians, excluding rival traders, discouraging immigration and settlement as far as possible, and determined to retain the territory as a sphere of British influence.

In 1834, the Reverend Jason Lee, a Methodist missionary from the United States, entered the field and was urged by McLoughlin to establish a mission in the Willamette valley. He also opened a branch station at The Dalles. Shortly afterwards the American Board of Commissioners for Foreign Missions, representing the Presbyterian, Congregational and Dutch Reformed Churches, had sent the Reverend Samuel Parker, a Presbyterian minister, and Dr. Marcus Whitman, a physician, to explore the Oregon country with a view to the early establishment of missions there. Their journey took them first to Walla Walla which, they decided, was the place for their mission. Then, while Parker went on to Fort Vancouver for the winter, Whitman returned to the United States for reinforcements.

When these arrived two mission stations were established, one at Waiilatpu, a few miles east of Walla Walla, and the other in the Nez Perce country at Lapwai on the Clearwater River. The Methodists extended their operations in 1840 by opening new missions at Nisqually on Puget Sound and Clatsop at the mouth of the Columbia.

As a general rule McLoughlin urged upon the American missionaries the wisdom of establishing their posts south of the Columbia since he felt that when the inevitable partition came, which could not be long delayed, Britain might well retain the country north of the river. With the same thought in mind the Roman Catholic missionaries, the Reverend Francois Norbert Blanchet and the Reverend Modeste Demers, who arrived from Quebec in November, 1838, were directed to establish their

missions in the Cowlitz valley north of the Columbia river. Blanchet, however, realised that most of his prospective parishioners
were across the river and with the tacit acquiescence of the Company he opened a mission in the Willamette Valley. At the same
time he wrote to his superiors in Quebec

> England and the United States have for several years been contesting
> relative to the occupancy of part of the territory of the Columbia.
> The former supposes that the Columbia is the boundary, while the
> latter are of the opinion that it is to be the 49th parallel, as to the
> east of the Rocky Mountains. According to the former hypothesis
> Cowlitz, Vancouver, and the most important establishments of the
> Company, except that of Walamette, will remain attached to British
> territory; while according to the second they will find themselves
> included in the possessions of the American Union. It seems that the
> question is to be decided before long.[1]

The Treaty of Oregon which effected the partition was signed
on June 15th, 1846, and the United States view prevailed, partly
because of American propaganda but largely because of American immigration to the Oregon country during the previous decade. In order to avoid a rush of American immigration to the
remaining territory with similar results the British government
set up the crown colony of Vancouver Island in 1849. As there
were no funds available for the administration of the new colony
it was suggested that the Hudson's Bay Company's chief factor at Victoria, James Douglas, should be appointed governor for
the time being. The office was given, however, to Richard Blanshard who had no experience in colonial administration but who
had held positions under the Colonial Office in the West Indies,
British Honduras and India. He arrived at his new post in Fort
Victoria on March 10th, 1850. As there had been no time for
organization, Blanshard found himself in a most unenviable position as a governor without a colony, and, even more serious, a
governor without a salary. Moreover, he soon clashed with

Douglas and in less than a year tendered his resignation and returned in disgust to England. Douglas himself was then appointed governor. In 1858, following the discovery of gold on the mainland, the crown colony of British Columbia was set up and Douglas was appointed governor on the understanding that he should divest himself of his interests in the Hudson's Bay Company. He remained as governor of both colonies until 1864. At that time Arthur Edward Kennedy was appointed governor of Vancouver Island, a post which he retained until the union of the colony with British Columbia in 1866. On the resignation of Douglas, who had been knighted in 1863, Frederick Seymour was appointed governor of British Columbia, and continued as governor of the united colonies until his death in 1869, when Anthony Musgrave replaced him. Musgrave remained in office until 1871 when British Columbia entered Confederation.

Within a few years of establishment as a colony, missionary societies in England began to regard the area as a promising field of work both in ministering to the white traders and settlers and in evangelizing the Indians. The agents of three societies appeared within a short time of each other; those sent by the Church Missionary Society (C.M.S.), the Society for the Propagation of the Gospel (S.P.G.), and the Colonial and Continental Church Society (C. & C.C.S.).

The C.M.S. was first made aware of the Pacific northwest as a potential sphere of work in 1819 when a member of the North West Fur Company suggested that the Indians beyond the Rocky Mountains were likely to respond to the preaching of the Gospel.[2] At that time nothing was done but in 1830 seven Indian boys from the region beyond the Rocky Mountains were being taught at the Red River Academy.[3] In 1856 the suggestion was renewed by Captain James Prevost of the Royal Navy who had just returned from the north Pacific and spoke of the evil influences of the white traders, urging that missionaries be sent to show the Indians the Christian way of life.[4] A few months later he was ordered back to the Pacific in command of H.M.S. *Satellite*, and offered free passage for a missionary, if he could sail at once.

To find someone at such short notice was a difficult under-taking but a man was forthcoming in the person of William Duncan who was at that time training for missionary work at the Highbury Training College for Schoolmasters, maintained by the C.M.S. After a dismissal service at the Church Missionary House Duncan sailed from Plymouth in the *Satellite* on December 23rd, arriving at Esquimalt June 13th, 1857. Fort Simpson, his ultimate destination, was still another five hundred miles north and the Hudson's Bay Company, who maintained a fort there, strongly opposed his going. They pointed out that as he could only go outside the fort at the risk of his life, and as the Indians would not be allowed to come in, there would be nothing he could do. Duncan persisted and was finally given a passage in a Company vessel arriving at his post on October 1st. Once there he visited the homes of the Tsimshian Indians assiduously, conducted Sunday services, organized a day school for the children and a night school for adults. It is probable, in spite of all his missionary efforts, that he shone chiefly as an administrator. Not long after his arrival he planned a Christian colony the objects of which he later set forth in a report to the Government.

1. To place all Christians, when they became wishful to be taught Christianity, out of the miasma of heathen life, and away from the deadening and enthralling influence of heathen customs.
2. To establish the Mission where we could effectively shut out intoxicating liquors, and keep liquors at bay.
3. To enable us to raise a barrier against the Indians visiting Victoria, except on lawful business.
4. That we might be able to assist the people thus gathered out to develop into a model community, and raise a Christian village,

THE CHRISTIAN VILLAGE OF METLACATLA.

*An engraving from The Columbia Mission Report, 1867*

from which the Native evangelists might go forth, and Christian truth radiate to every tribe around.

5. That we might gather such a community around us, whose moral and religious training and bent of life might render it safe and proper to impart secular instruction.

6. That we might be able to break up all tribal distinctions and animosities, and cement all who came to us, from whatever tribe, into one common brotherhood.

7. That we might also place ourselves in a position to set up and establish the supremacy of law, teach loyalty to the Queen, conserve the peace of the country around, and ultimately develop our settlement into a municipality with its Native Corporation.[5]

The place selected for the experiment was Metlakatla, some seventeen miles south of Fort Simpson, which had formerly been the home of the Indians before the establishment of the fort. The colony came into being in the summer of 1862 when Duncan and some three hundred and fifty Indians moved to the new location. Before long a flourishing community was in full swing.

Duncan, as we shall see later, was a peculiar man, increasingly unorthodox in his theological ideas, and more than a little of a megalomaniac. As evidence of the former it may be pointed out that he made no attempt to give the Scriptures to the Indians in their own tongue, nor would he permit them to be admitted to the Holy Communion, lest they make of it a fetish. In all his letters to Governor Douglas, Duncan insisted that he looked to the time when his Indian community should be self-sustaining and self-governing but his actions give the lie to his apparent desire for their autonomy. Moreover, like so many nineteenth century missionaries, he assumed that Christianity and the outward conventions of western civilization must necessarily go hand in hand, and therefore sought to compel the Indians to conform to white manners of dress and housing. When the first Bishop of Caledonia visited Metlakatla at the end of 1879 he was greatly

*Right Reverend George Hills, first Bishop of British Columbia.*

Reverend Edward Cridge

William Duncan

Reverend W. Burton Crickmer

Canon J. B. Good

impressed by the decorum and orderly behaviour of the community. It was not long, however, before he discovered the real reason and wrote to the Church Missionary Society:

> Inwardly I exclaimed What God hath wrought! But it would be wrong to suppose that the love of God alone impelled them all. All, without reasonable cause to the contrary, are expected to attend the public services. A couple of policemen, as a matter of routine, are in uniform, and this is an indication that loitering during service hours is against proper civil order. This wholesome restraint is possible in these early stages of the corporate life of the community. *At present one strong will is supreme.* To resist it, every Indian feels, would be as impossible as to stop the tides. This righteous autocracy is as much feared by the ungodly as it is respected by the faithful.[6]

Nor did Duncan intend to tolerate interference or competition from other missionaries. Five times the C.M.S. sent out clergy to work in the area and each in turn found it impossible to remain in the community with the eccentric lay missionary. In the summer of 1860 Duncan had visited Victoria and had drawn up recommendations for the Indian settlement there. As he was not well at the time it was suggested that he should move to Victoria and take part in the Indian work there[7] but this curtailment of his powers and influence evidently did not appeal to Duncan and he remained in the north.

That same year the Reverend L. S. Tugwell was sent out by the C.M.S. but returned within two years, to be followed in 1864 by the Reverend R. R. A. Doolan who was soon to be despatched by Duncan to start a new mission on the Nass River. Shortly afterwards Doolan's health failed and he returned to England. In 1865 the Reverend F. B. Gribbell was sent out but soon withdrew to undertake colonial work at Victoria under the Bishop. 1867 saw the Reverend Robert Tomlinson continuing the work on the Nass River. He remained for several years, carrying on the work begun by Doolan.

William Henry Collison came to Metlakatla in 1873 but as he was a layman and evidently deferred to Duncan he was permitted to remain until 1876 when, of his own volition and with the permission of the C.M.S., he moved to Massett. Originally it had been intended that he should remain at Metlakatla enabling Duncan to move further afield. In 1877 the Reverend A. J. Hall was sent out by the Society as priest-in-charge of Metlakatla but before long he too was requested by Duncan to undertake other work on Vancouver Island. He then served for many years as missionary at Alert Bay, translating parts of the Bible and Prayer Book into the Indian tongue. So the unusual story continued until the crisis came which led Duncan to sever his connections both with the Church Missionary Society and the British Empire, and to move with many of his followers to Alaska. That part of the story we shall take up later.

It is time now to return to Victoria to meet the third and last of the Hudson's Bay Company's chaplains on the Pacific coast. Edward Cridge, who was later to create an uproar in the Church in British Columbia, was a pronounced Evangelical. After taking his degree from St. Peter's College, (Peterhouse), Cambridge, he had served for some time as a schoolmaster at the Endowed Grammar School, South Molton, Devon, while at the same time acting as tutor to the children of the Vicar of North Molton. In February, 1848, he was ordained Deacon in Norwich Cathedral, and advanced to the priesthood in the same place on Sunday, February 24th, 1850. He next appeared as incumbent, which would seem to mean curate-in-charge, of Christ Church, Stratford, London.

In the summer of 1854 he was informed that the chaplaincy of the Hudson's Bay Company at Victoria was vacant and told that if he applied for it he would probably be appointed. By his own account:

On Wednesday, August 30th, 1854, the Vicar of West Ham told me that the Chaplaincy of Vancouver's Island was vacant and thought that if I applied I might very likely obtain it, for which purpose he would use his influence on my behalf: he wished me to give him some notion of my mind on the matter before the evening as Capt. Pelly who had informed him of the vacancy had also told him that the Hudson's Bay Company wished to make the appointment immediately. After . . . some further conversation . . . I consented to become a candidate. My past experience in educational matters seemed to them a strong qualification. I was led however to this decision not only by their judgment but also by the consideration that God might perhaps by this means be answering my prayers and petitions. . . .[8]

References were secured and interviews with the Hudson's Bay Company followed. Cridge was offered the appointment if he would agree to sail at once. After some hesitation he and his fiancee agreed to do so. On Thursday, September 14th, his marriage to Mary Winnell took place at West Ham Parish Church, and they sailed together from Gravesend the following Wednesday on board the *Marquis of Bute*. After a long and tiring voyage they reached Victoria on April 1st, 1855. As the parsonage was not ready Cridge and his wife were accommodated for a time in the fort whose large and airy rooms, he said, were a pleasant change from the cramped quarters of the ship.

His first services were held in the messroom of the fort with no organ or choir to lead the singing. The District Church as it was called was in course of erection when Cridge arrived and was a small wooden building put up by the Hudson's Bay Company almost on the site of the present cathedral and named Christ Church after the church which the chaplain had served in London. It was opened in August, 1856. In addition to his work there Cridge held services at Craigflower School, and sometimes on visiting naval vessels. In return, he was occasionally able to persuade visiting naval chaplains to preach for him at the District Church. Writing many years afterwards of those early days, Cridge said,

> I know not what the population of Victoria might be at that time, though I think two hundred would be the outside; the population of the whole Island being about 600. You could, I think, count the houses on each side of the four principal streets, Government, Fort, Yates, Johnson, on the fingers of one hand. I remember three on James Bay side, to reach which, there being no bridge to connect with Government Street, you had to go round where the Church of Our Lord now stands.[9]

Three years after his arrival Cridge was able to write to the Colonial and Continental Church Society telling of the rapid growth of population on account of the Cariboo gold rush and appealing for more clergy to minister to the greatly increased numbers.

> Three months ago the outside population of Victoria was 4,000 nearly all encamped in white tents of every size and form. It is confidently expected that before winter we shall count the thousands of our population, not by units but by tens. How many are gone to the diggings I know not; some weeks ago the number was said to be more than 3,000, and they are going up via Victoria, by steamer, two or three times a week, besides canvas and other craft; and some overland. The river [Fraser] is not yet sufficiently fallen for extensive operations, when it is, it is universally supposed that the rush will far surpass that to California or Australia in former days. An extensive merchant told me this morning that the people were leaving San Francisco in crowds. . . .
>
> I feel sure that the people might be won if immediate efforts were made. Two clergymen ought to be sent out immediately—one to Victoria and one to the diggings. Who is to send them? I write in the first instance to the Colonial Church and School Society. In our present unsettled state it is scarcely to be expected that the colany [sic] can do much, though, doubtless, by and by it will be able to do almost everything for itself, . . . [10]

In the same letter he spoke of open air services held for the miners which, he said, had met with a very satisfactory response, and of an episcopal visit paid to Victoria in the summer of 1857 by Bishop Scott of Oregon who confirmed twenty candidates.

As with so many other gold rushes the excitement soon died down and numbers dwindled, but in response to Cridge's appeal the Colonial and Continental Church Society sent out the Reverend W. Burton Crickmer, M.A. (Oxon.), who arrived at Victoria in H.M.S. *Plumper* on Christmas Day, 1858, having been licensed by the Bishop of London to minister to "British residents in British Columbia sojourning in the Hudson [sic] Bay Company's territory of Victoria, Vancouver's Island."[11]

By March, 1859 Crickmer was established at Fort Langley (Derby) and almost immediately wrote to Governor Douglas asking for the enlargement of the parsonage. Having dealt with the parsonage problem he again wrote to the Governor announcing that the new Church of St. John the Divine, Langley, would be opened on May 1st, 1859. When, in 1858, the colony of British Columbia was erected, Douglas hoped that Langley would become the capital but Colonel R. C. Moody, officer commanding the Royal Engineers in the colony, felt that New Westminster offered a better site. The Governor's will prevailed for the time being and the proclamation constituting the new colony was actually read at Langley. Before long, however, the natural advantages of New Westminster were realized; it was further from the international boundary, had a better waterfront, and was nearer the mouth of the Fraser. "There can be no doubt," wrote Professor A. S. Morton, "that the Governor erred in his choice, and that Col. Moody's eye saw true."[12] None-the-less, the residents of Langley did not give up without a struggle and on August 26th, 1859, Crickmer penned a strong appeal to the Governor for the retention of Langley as the capital. The cause was lost, however, and Langley declined. In consequence, the population decreased, Crickmer was transferred to Yale, and the church which he had built was abandoned and later moved across the river to Maple Ridge.

The first priest of the Society for the Propagation of the Gospel to reach Victoria was the Reverend Richard Dowson who with his wife had sailed from London on October 15th, 1858. They arrived in Victoria in the following February, and found the town to be "a strange assemblage of wooden houses, with a mixed population of every nation, numbering about 1,500: everything very dear, about three or four times the English price; and labour of every kind exceedingly high."[13] As there was no accommodation to be had in Victoria, Dowson and his wife went to stay with Captain Langford and his family who occupied a large farm near the community which bears his name.

Within a fortnight of their arrival Dowson was able to undertake a voyage of exploration in one of the Hudson's Bay Company's vessels. Leaving Victoria, the ship sailed round the southern tip of the Island and reached Nanaimo which the missionary described as follows: "the village or town of Nanaimo is a most miserable affair, simply the wood cleared away and the small wooden houses without the slightest attempt at design or beauty sprinkled as it were amongst the mud and stumps."[14] From Nanaimo they went to Fort Rupert at the northern tip of the Island and then on to Fort Simpson where Dowson met William Duncan, the C.M.S. schoolmaster. Perhaps it is significant that Dowson made no comment about him beyond the fact that he had seen him.

On his return Dowson was still unable to find suitable accommodation and had to rest content with "a dilapidated school house belonging to the colony . . . about four miles from Victoria."[15] This was probably the Craigflower school where Cridge had occasionally held services. The building still stands where Admirals Road crosses the Gorge. Dowson continued his work there for almost a year but was compelled to return to England in February, 1860, on account of his wife's illness.

The Reverend James Gammage, the second of the S.P.G. missionaries, reached Esquimalt on April 11th, 1859, and had a similar story to tell about difficulties in the new colony. For drinking water he had to pay sixpence a pail, for butter three shillings a pound, and for milk one shilling a quart, while servants could not be procured even by the Governor. His first few weeks were spent in a journey through the Fraser river district as far as Lytton. After pausing at Hope where, to his regret, only eight people came to the service, he passed on to Yale where he was completely unable to persuade the miners to attend a service. He walked to Lytton where he found some twenty houses and a population of thirty souls. On the Sunday he had a service in the morning to which twelve people came, and another in the afternoon with a congregation of nine. From Lytton he went to Cayoosh, later known as Lillooet, but was not able to hold a service, and so back to Douglas. In undertaking this pilgrimage Gammage became the first Anglican priest to hold services in the Cariboo. The Oblate order of the Roman Church had sent missionaries through the district in 1841, and then permanently established themselves there twenty years later.

---

1 Carl Landerholm, (Trans.) *Notices and Voyages of the Famed Quebec Mission to the Pacific Northwest,* Oregon Historical Society, Portland, 1956, p. 23.
2 Eugene Stock, *The History of the Church Missionary Society,* London, C.M.S., 1899, I, p. 245.
3 *Ibid.* II, p. 611.
4 Article in the *Church Missionary Intelligencer,* 1856, p. 166-168.
5 E. Stock, op. cit., II, p. 617.
A similar recommendation was drawn up by Duncan for the Indian settlement at Victoria and submitted to Governor Douglas in June,

1860, after Duncan had visited the capital. The original of this document is in the Provincial Archives, Victoria, B.C.

6 E. Stock, op. cit., III, p. 251.

7 *Columbia Mission Report*, 1860, p. 35.

8 The diaries of Edward Cridge are in the Provincial Archives, Victoria, B.C.

9 *Victoria Daily Colonist*, December 22nd, 1907.

10 Letter to the Colonial and Continental Church Society, July 5th, 1858. Copy in the Archives of the Ecclesiastical Province of British Columbia, Vancouver, B.C.

11 Letter to C. & C.C.S., January 6th, 1859. Copy in the Archives of the Ecclesiastical Province of B.C., Vancouver.

12 A. S. Morton, *A History of the Canadian West to 1870-1*, Thomas Nelson & Sons, London, (no date) p. 776.

13 Report from the Rev. Richard Dowson to the S.P.G., February 4th, 1859. Microfilm of transcript in Archives of the Ecclesiastical Province of B.C.

14 Letter to S.P.G., April 4th, 1859. Transcript in the Provincial Archives, Victoria, B.C.

15 loc cit.

# 3

# The First Bishop

ONE of the difficulties experienced by the Church in other parts of the world was the lack of a bishop in the formative stages of her growth and development. Perhaps this was nowhere more marked than in the American colonies where for well over a century the Church was without episcopal leadership. In British Columbia this difficulty was avoided through the generosity of Miss (later Baroness) Angela Burdett Coutts who in the summer of 1858 wrote to the Archbishop of Canterbury offering the sum of fifteen thousand pounds as an episcopal endowment. This was gladly accepted by Archbishop Sumner, and by Sir Edward Bulwer Lytton, the Colonial Secretary, who transmitted the news to Governor Douglas in Victoria. The letter was duly acknowledged by the Governor who said, "A more acceptable gift than this munificent donation, or one calculated to diffuse a greater amount of public good, could hardly have been devised and I beg, on behalf of the Colony, to offer most grateful thanks to the generous lady whose name and beneficence will be commemorated in the records of the country."[1]

The occasion of this magnificent gift seems to have been the discovery of gold and the resulting rush of prospectors into what soon became the crown colony of British Columbia. According to Douglas, "gold was first found on the Thompson River by an Indian a quarter of a mile below Nicomen. . . . The Indian was taking a drink out of the river; having no vessel he was quaffing from the stream when he perceived a shining pebble which he picked up, and it proved to be gold. The whole tribe forthwith began to collect the glittering metal. This was probably in 1856."[2]

Shortly after this discovery thousands of miners and prospectors, largely from California, poured into the unorganized mainland territory. Governor Douglas watched the influx from Victoria with mounting anxiety, fully aware of the difficulties which could ensue if law and order were not maintained. Actually his authority did not extend to the mainland but feeling that the emergency justified his disregard of such a technicality Douglas issued regulations in December, 1857, to control gold mining. These regulations, or misunderstandings concerning them, were responsible for a disturbance known as the Ned McGowan War, and this, strangely enough, led to the holding of the first Anglican service on the lower mainland after the establishment of the new colony.

At the end of 1858, Ned McGowan, a notorious character, fell foul of the law. The report which reached Fort Langley indicated that a serious insurrection might follow which would require military aid for its suppression. Colonel R. C. Moody, commanding the Royal Engineers, set out with a small detachment, accompanied by Judge Begbie, to deal with the situation. He discovered at Yale that affairs were not as serious as supposed although had he not undertaken the expedition conditions might have deteriorated. The day following Moody's arrival at Yale was a Sunday and he invited all in the vicinity to join with him in a service to be held in the Court House. Here is his own description of that service on January 16th, 1859.

The day after my arrival at Fort Yale was a Sunday and I sent round to invite everybody to meet me at Divine Service in the Court House. It was the first time in British Columbia that the Liturgy of our Church was read .... To *me* God in his mercy granted this privilege. The room was crowded full of Hill's Bar men as well as others, old grey-bearded men, young eager-eyed men, stern middle-aged men, of all nations knelt with me before the throne of Grace. . . . When it was concluded, I gave them a few words in which I must have expressed my affection for them, and I prayed God to bless them all and prosper them all in their labours . . . . I have since heard that at one of the Bars a Log Hut is now building as a Church, being built by the miners themselves, no Clergyman is there among them. Oh! for some of England's Gentlemen, young and ardent as Ministers of God's Words. How many Curates there are of ample private means to whom pay would be nothing . . . . Let a few such men come here and take post against the enemy of these Miners' souls . . . they need someone to dwell among them as clergymen, and the Missionaries to send among them must be of a particular stamp.[3]

It was to meet the needs of the new colony as well as to minister to those already resident on Vancouver Island that the new diocese was established. Almost immediately after the endowment had been set up the appointment to the see was offered to the Reverend George Hills, M.A. (Dunelm.), who was at that time Vicar of Great Yarmouth. The invitation was probably extended on the suggestion of Miss Burdett Coutts herself. The Reverend J. B. Good, one of the early missionaries, wrote in his unpublished autobiography,

Miss Burdett Coutts . . . had long held Bishop Hills, when he was the widely known Vicar of Yarmouth, in her esteem and confidence, and it was understood that she was the moving cause of his selection for this new and far off post of duty.[4]

Hills protested that he would gladly see the post given to one more suited but his objections were overcome and he was consecrated in Westminster Abbey on St. Matthias' Day, 1859. A slight hitch occurred afterwards which marred the new Bishop's entry upon his work. According to custom, the offering at the consecration service was given to the S.P.G. for work in the new Bishop's diocese. The Bishop, however, had appointed as his commissary the Reverend John Garrett, M.A., Vicar of St. Paul near Penzance, who insisted that the moneys should have been paid into a special Columbia Mission Fund which he controlled. Garrett proved to be something of a nuisance both to the Society and to some of the Bishop's supporters. After a few years his connection with the fund ceased and no further reference to his activities is found.

The new Bishop spent the summer of 1859 in England enlisting support and raising funds for his diocese. He had the support of the S.P.G. but in addition established the Columbia Mission Fund mentioned above which, in its first three years, provided more than £23,000 for general purposes. Among the clergy recruited by the Bishop were the Reverend R. J. Dundas, M.A. (Oxon.), who had been one of his curates at Great Yarmouth, and the Reverend John Sheepshanks, M.A. (Cantab.), who was an assistant curate under the famed Dr. Hook at Leeds Parish Church. They were the first to sail and reached Victoria in the summer of 1859. Two others, the Reverend A. C. Garrett, B.A., with his wife and two small children, and the Reverend R. L. Lowe, sailed in the *Heather Bell* in October of that year for the long voyage round the Cape to British Columbia.

Dundas remained in Victoria, there to become the incumbent of St. John's, the second parish in Victoria, for which the Bishop had an iron church built in England at a cost of £2,400 and shipped out to its new location near where the Hudson's Bay Company's store now stands. Sheepshanks went to New Westminster, looking forward to his new work among the miners and settlers. When he came to his new charge it was to discover that there was no church, no endowment for his stipend, and no house in which to live. Making the best of circumstances and showing great willingness to adapt himself to them, he took possession of a log hut which had been abandoned by a couple of miners. The first service was held on Sunday, September 2nd, and for it Sheepshanks obtained the use of the Custom House. About seven or eight men, and no women, put in a shame-faced appearance. Before long the congregation outgrew the Custom House and services were held in the larger quarters afforded by the Court House. At length there was talk of a church building. The land on which the rector's shack stood was acquired by Crown grant and there was a "bee" for the clearing of the ground. Many came to put in a day's work, bringing with them shovels and pickaxes to remove stumps and to make a pathway from the road up to the church property.

The Bishop himself left England on November 17th, 1859, after a farewell service at St. James' Church, Piccadilly, when he preached on the text, "Brethren, pray for us," (I Thess. 5. 25). The service was followed by a meeting of the Columbia Mission at the Mansion House under the chairmanship of the Lord Mayor of London. Bishop Hills arrived in Victoria on January 6th, the Feast of the Epiphany, and was entranced by the physical surrounding but anxious for the state of the Church. In writing to the Secretary of the S.P.G. just after he arrived he commented, "How important is our work. The Church of England here is in a feeble state. Had it been left long so it would almost have been trampled out."[5]

In May, 1860, a few months after he had arrived, Bishop Hills set out on a tour of the mainland, going first to New Westminster where, on May 22nd, he laid the foundation stone of Holy Trinity Church. While there he visited Langley and saw the church which had been erected by the Reverend W. B. Crickmer.

On Whitsunday, May 27th, the Bishop took part in the services at New Westminster, and celebrated Holy Communion at the camp of the Royal Engineers where there were but six communicants. "This is sad," was the Bishop's comment in his journal.[6] During his stay at New Westminster he also accompanied Colonel Moody on an excursion to Douglas where, after being met by the Reverend James Gammage, the S.P.G. missionary there, he inspected the ground set apart for a church site. Soon afterwards the Bishop, accompanied by Dundas and Sheepshanks, set out for Hope with the Governor. He was greatly intrigued by the flat-bottomed stern-wheeler, and spoke highly of the service on board. In a report later he described his experiences.

> About forty miles from the mouth of the Harrison we came upon the mining bars: Hudson's Bar, Last Chance Bar, Blue Nose, Manhattan, Cornish. Some are sandbanks stretching out into the stream, covered at the high seasons with water, as at present: dry from August to March. Some are the side banks of the river which they dig away, scoop out, and extract gold. The upper earth is removed first, then, about four feet down, is a deposit of black sand in which is the gold. To get this upper coat away the miner brings a stream of water . . . which he plies in a hose with a strong jet, and washes away vast quantities in a short time till he gets to the "pay dirt".[7]

At length Hope was reached and on June 3rd, Trinity Sunday, the Bishop held a service assisted by the Reverend A. St. D. F. Pringle, M.A., another of the recently arrived S.P.G. missionaries. There were from forty to fifty present including the

Governor and the Chief Justice. As there was yet no church the service was held in Pringle's room. It was followed by a celebration at which, the Bishop noted with obvious regret, there were but five people present. While in Hope the Bishop was urged to provide a school for the Indians and after conferring with the church wardens, Messrs. O'Reilly and Hotchkins, he went on his way.

Pringle was not only quite active in his own pastoral work but in local affairs generally and in the running of a reading room or church institute. Such institutes were a familiar part of many parishes in the nineteenth century and were felt to be particularly important in such places as Hope where the population consisted largely of single men whose only other diversions were the many saloons. Pringle, therefore, collected funds to buy a building which was opened on December 1st, 1859, as the Fort Hope Reading Room and Library.

From Hope the Bishop and his party went upstream to Yale, delayed for a time because the Indians who were to have taken him in a canoe failed to appear, and when they did so were the worse for liquor. They returned, sober, the next day and the voyage of fifteen miles was accomplished in eight hours after which, said the traveller, "we were hospitably received by Mr. Crickmer and his estimable lady,"[8] the Crickmers having moved there from Langley just before the Bishop's visit.

Soon after his arrival Crickmer had obtained the use of a store which he had fitted up for use as a temporary church. This building the Bishop dedicated on June 10th, 1860. Commenting on the service he went on to say,

He [Crickmer] has a melodeon which the people have purchased. The musical part of the service was very creditably performed considering most present had never before heard chanting. About forty persons were present, amongst others, the Governor and Col. Moody. The usual congregation is not above twelve or fifteen, so this was a large representation . . . . The Holy Communion was celebrated in the morning: there were but three communicants.[9]

After almost a fortnight in the vicinity of Yale the Bishop, accompanied by Crickmer, went further up the river to Spuzzum and thence to Boston Bar and Lytton where they pitched their tents on a flat overlooking the Fraser and Thompson rivers. Two services were held on the Sunday at the Court House and they were well attended. Said the Bishop,

> Considering the population, and the character of the people, as regards nation and creed, the services were hearty: we had much singing; and the cards containing ten hymns distributed answered well. I preached in the morning upon the happy results of true religion and in the evening upon prayer. There was great attention. In the morning all but three were in shirt-sleeves; no one but Captain Ball and my own party had Prayer Books.[10]

The party remained only a day or so in Lytton and then continued up the Fraser River to Lillooet. All along the route the missionaries met a great many Indians, most of whom were kindly disposed, and some of whom had an inkling of the Christian Faith from the Roman Catholic priests who had passed through the country at an earlier date. Speaking of one such meeting with the Fountain Indians, the Bishop wrote,

> At half-past six they began to assemble. As they came up, all advanced to shake hands, and many of them made the sign of the cross on the face and breast. The children too were brought, and their dirty little hands were all held out to be touched. They then seated themselves in a ring round Mr. Sheepshanks and myself. Every now and then one would start up and shout towards the village, for some stray Indian who had not yet come; and once an Indian darted off and returned with several. There was one very old man, with silvery hair: he was the village chief; his name was Isualtoe. Two others were prominent in repeating what was said, and in interpreting. I addressed them; told them who I was; why I had come; showed them the Bible; told them it was the word of God; we knew what it contained; they did not; there was a message of love to them as

32

IRON CHURCH AND MISSION HOUSE IN COLUMBIA.

*An engraving from the Columbia Mission Occasional Paper, June, 1860.*

well as to us; we wished them to know this message from their heavenly Father; . . . I then spoke to them of God, . . . pointed out that all were sinners, . . . and then told of the love and work of Christ . . . . These poor people frequently became much moved; discussed vehemently what was said—so I had occasionally to pause —and I believe received true impressions, notwithstanding stammering lips.

Mr. Sheepshanks followed and made an effective address, after which I again spoke to them, . . . Some of the townspeople came and listened and were interested. Miners stopped as they passed, and Chinese had an opportunity of being reminded there was a God. For two hours the interest did not for an instant flag. None removed till we suggested that it was time to go to rest. Then one by one all came and shook hands, and still lingered till we ourselves left the spot.[11]

After a week or more among the Indians the Bishop and his party went back to Lytton, and on to Boston Bar and Hope. Of this journey Sheepshanks has left a description.

First came the tall, grave, dignified Bishop. So tall was he, and so long of limb, that riding on a big horse, if he dropped his whip to the ground, he could pick it up while still in the saddle.

Next came the young presbyter [Sheepshanks himself], his chaplain, by no means so correct in his appearance, in wide-awake, serge coat, clerical tie—which he never abandoned, corduroy trousers, and hob-nailed boots.

Next came the "faithful William," the Bishop's servant, not much relishing the rough work of missionary travel, and the cavalcade wound up with two packed horses, and the packer.

The Bishop was always kindly and considerate; but sometimes his English clerical ideas of propriety were a little disturbed. The young chaplain had a "way," the same "way" which in Mr. Sam Weller so disturbed the equanimity of Mr. John Smauker, of putting his hands in his pockets and whistling as he went. It appears that this fidgetted the stately Bishop and shocked his sense of proprieties. So one day the reproof fell: "I cannot think how you can indulge in that habit of whistling. It is so undignified. I might say so unclerical." There was a twinkle in the chaplain's eye, and a smile flickered round his mouth. But he had too genuine a respect for his superior to make any reply, and a pleasant conversation ensued. But a while afterwards, perhaps after the midday meal, the chaplain would strangely find himself half a mile behind the others, and lo! again the sombre forest would re-echo with the popular airs of the period.[12]

When the party reached Hope services were held there and a fortnight spent in work among the Indians and miners. The Bishop returned to Victoria, having travelled approximately 826 miles in a little less than three months. As for Sheepshanks, when he reached New Westminster again he found the church almost completed. It would seat about three hundred people and was dedicated in honour of the Holy Trinity on December 2nd, 1860, only to be burned down five years later.

As we read this account of beginnings in missionary work we may well pause to think of its effect upon those immediately involved, upon Bishop Hills, fresh from his populous parish with large congregations and a staff of assistant curates; upon John Sheepshanks who had just left his curacy in a large north-country parish; or upon Pringle at Christ Church, Hope, in circumstances so different from those of Christ Church, Paddington. Probably their impressions were threefold: the primitive nature of buildings and roads, the small population, and the vast distances to be travelled. The churches, where they existed at all, were small wooden structures but in most instances they remained to be built, and the comment of one missionary is revealing. "The houses and stores," he said, "are all after the American fashion; but the Church gave the place an English look!"[13] The population though small was diverse with representatives from many nations and creeds, including Indians and Chinese, but with the exception of the Indians, consisting almost wholly of men. There were practically no women in the colony and this gave rise to an interesting experiment in immigration as we shall see later. As for the distances—relatives and friends of missionaries must have smiled in polite disbelief at the stories they received of distances and modes of travel. In England, a trip to London could be the event of a lifetime, but in British Columbia one might set out for Hope or Yale, or even the remote Cariboo without turning a hair. One might travel by river steamer or canoe, on horseback or on foot, and most journeys required a combination of two or three of these methods. The Fraser was no sluggish stream like the Ouse or the Cam, nor even a peaceful river like the Thames or the Trent, but a mightly rushing flood with rapids and whirlpools and hidden rocks all waiting to lure the unwary or inexperienced traveller to a quick and watery grave. Roads were no better, mere trails through the bush with potholes and fallen trees or precarious paths along the mountainside with a sheer drop to the river below. If we are sometimes tempted to criticize these pioneers of the Faith for what they did or did not do we may also sympathise with them for the hardships and loneliness they endured.

We have noticed once or twice Bishop Hills' distress that so few people came to join in the celebrations of Holy Communion but this was not altogether surprising. There were relatively few communicants and, moreover, the Church was rarely of prime importance to the settlers and transient miners. The practice of religion, if thought of at all, was regarded as a luxury to be left until the stern business of the moment was completed. Further, those who came to the colony, as to other frontier settlements, were often men who came to escape what to them were the cramped and confining circumstances of older societies, among them the ordinary demands of Christian life and worship.

Then, too, there was a changing attitude towards the Holy Communion throughout the Anglican world. At the Reforma- tion, Cranmer and others had hedged the service about with rubrics intended to increase the numbers of participants at Holy Communion but the effect had been only to reduce the number of celebrations because there were no communicants. Hence, in most churches until the middle of the nineteenth century or even later it was customary to administer the Holy Communion only at Christmas, Easter, Whitsuntide, and Michaelmas. Bishop Hills, on the other hand, had evidently been influenced by the Oxford Movement or Catholic Revival which began in 1833 and which saw the Eucharist as the central act of Christian worship to be celebrated every Sunday, or even every day of the week. He was therefore anxious to encourage his people to the more frequent reception of the Sacrament, but old customs die hard as witness the resistance of a congregation to a new hymn tune or a revised pointing of the psalter. The change has come, however, and now there is scarcely a church without a weekly communion provided there is a priest available to celebrate it.

1 Letter to the Colonial Secretary, December 28th, 1858. From printed records in the Provincial Archives, Victoria, B. C.
2 F. W. Howay & E. O. S. Scholefield, *British Columbia*, S. J. Clarke Publishing Co., Vancouver, 1914, II, p. 10.
3 "First Impressions: Letter of Col. R. C. Moody, R.E., to Arthur Blackwood, Feb. 1st, 1859," *British Columbia Historical Quarterly*, Jan.-Apr., 1951, pp. 85-107.
4 "The Utmost Bounds of the West," by the Rev. J. B. Good; original manuscript in the Provincial Archives, Victoria, B. C.
5 *The Occasional Paper*, June, 1860; published by the Columbia Mission. Copy in the Archives of the Ecclesiastical Province of British Columbia, Vancouver, B. C.
6 *Columbia Mission Report*, 1860, p.34.
7 *Ibid.*, p.36.
8 *Ibid.*, p.41.
9 loc. cit.
10 *Ibid.*, p.59.
11 *Ibid.*, pp.64-65.
12 D. Wallace Duthie, *A Bishop in the Rough*, Smith, Elder, London, 1909, p. 45.
13 *Columbia Mission Report*, 1861, p.30.

4

# Miners and
# Missionaries

THE first few years of any missionary enterprise are necessarily years of surveying and expansion, investigation and experiment, before permanent centres can be established. This was no less the case in British Columbia. A number of churches were built in centres which had only passing importance, and before long had ceased to exist entirely.

We have already seen Derby as an instance of this rise and decline. Another such centre was Douglas whose location at the head of Harrison Lake was of particular importance in the early days of the Cariboo gold rush. At that time one of the routes to the Cariboo, and that encouraged at first by Governor Douglas himself, was up Harrison Lake and the Lillooet river to what is now Creekside, over the summit to Anderson Lake, Seton Lake, and Lillooet, and thence by way of Pavilion to Clinton and the Cariboo. Property was secured in Douglas and a church and parsonage built. St. Mark's Church, "a very pretty one,"[1] was consecrated by the Bishop on May 13th, 1862 with a packed congregation including many Indians and miners but, he said, "Sunday is as busy a day as any other; stores are open, wagons are plying, mules are packing, exactly as on other days. . . . Such are the difficulties with which our clergy have to deal."[2] Perhaps even this was not the greatest difficulty for only a year after the opening of the church the famed Cariboo Road through the Fraser canyon from Yale to Lytton was completed and Port Douglas ceased to have any *raison d'etre*. Writing to the S.P.G. in July, 1863, Gammage could clearly see the future and suggested that the mission, if continued, should be addressed primarily to the native population. Actually, however, it was closed altogether. The church was later removed to Chilliwack, rebuilt, and re-dedicated to St. Thomas, on November 6th, 1873.

The Bishop's main concern after having seen the country for himself was to secure missionaries who might man the various centres. Among these selected was the Reverend R. C. Lundin Brown, M.A., who went to Lillooet. Very little seems to be known of him, beyond the fact that he wrote a prize-winning essay on British Columbia in 1863, and published a pamphlet entitled *The Dead in Christ*, at Wiesbaden, in 1868. He came to Lillooet in 1861 and was responsible for the building of the church there in 1862.

Brown was also responsible, though indirectly, for another interesting if not unique development in missionary history, the despatch of the "bride ships" to bring about a more equitable balance of sexes in British Columbia. With the discovery of gold the population had risen rapidly but consisted almost entirely of men. There were very few women. Word of the situation was brought to the annual meeting of the Columbia Mission in London, on February 27th, 1862, when an appeal was read from the Reverend R. C. Lundin Brown, in the following terms:

Dozens of men have told me they would gladly marry if they could. I was speaking one evening on the subject of the dearth of females and mentioned my intention of writing to beg that a plan of emigration may be set on foot; whereupon one member of the company immediately exclaimed, "Then, sir, I pre-empt a wife," and another and another, all round the circle of those listening to me earnestly exclaimed the same. Fancy the idea of pre-empting a wife! Yet, I assure you this touches the root of the greatest blessing which can now be conferred upon this Colony from home. Think of the 600,000 more women at home than there are men, and then think what society must be here. Churches may be and must be built, our faithful witness must be borne for holiness and virtue, but where there is no wedded life, churchgoing must be difficult, because morality is almost impossible. . . .[3]

The Bishop's commissary, who presented the report, went on to say that he had made some preliminary enquiries about a plan of emigration and the idea was enthusiastically supported by the Bishop of Oxford. As a result the Columbia Emigration Society came into being.

Through the agency of the society, girls and women from orphanages and poor houses were to be sent out to British Columbia where they would be employed in domestic service until they received the anticipated offers of marriage. In April, 1862, the first contingent of wives-to-be left England, and in June a further sixty set out in the steamer *Tynemouth*. Thirty-six more arrived in Victoria on the *Robert Lowe* in January, 1863. Many of them were married soon after arrival or went into service but, in the words of one historian,

A certain proportion went quickly to the bad and, from appearances, had been there before. Taken as a whole, the venture was a success but it was a delicate undertaking and, while deserving respect for the benevolent motive inspiring it, and for the good actually accomplished, it may be doubted whether such a method is to be recommended for supplying the wants of a new colony.[4]

Life was far from simple for the missionary clergy. Funds for buildings and stipends were not always forthcoming. There were many who regarded the Church and her agents with undisguised disdain to be ignored or taken advantage of as occasion seemed to require. On the other hand there were those who, regardless of their own attitude to the Church or the conventions with which it was identified, were moved to admiration for the clergy and lay workers who had come to these wild areas and who would rough it with the best or worst of them. Two incidents which took place during the summer of 1862 serve to show, on the one hand, the infrequent hostility of the miners and others, and on the other, the implicit respect for Christian conviction which could show itself on occasion.

The first incident took place at William's Lake at the time of the races and was described by Dundas who came there with the Bishop and Sheepshanks.

> On my going [to the local restaurant] to make preparations for service, one of the three proprietors came to me and advised that we should "quit preaching" today, there were so many "loafers" and drunken men about that we should certainly be interrupted, perhaps insulted. I said I was quite sure the Bishop would not consent to forego the service. . . . But the man was obstinate. He raised objection, and I saw clearly enough that his sole object was to prevent the service partly because its being held in or outside his house would to a certain extent interfere with a paying morning for business and partly because he did not wish to be identified too closely with parsons and their doings . . . . So I told him that never yet, from end to end of British Columbia, had a clergyman been compelled to forego a service on a Sunday for fear of interruption—not even among the gambling saloons of Cariboo . . . .
>
> The Bishop on my return to the house was greatly annoyed, but there was no help for it. We held our service in another house, in an inconvenient place, and had for a congregation five persons to whom the Bishop preached . . . .[5]

The other story came also from Dundas' pen and concerned

the lingering death from tuberculosis of a miner named Emery. He had not been a particularly devout man but the Bishop had visited him often and at the last he "accepted the Gospel tidings of pardon and peace."[6] Dundas was with him when he died and, thinking that the Bishop who had seen so much of him would like to be present at the funeral, sent word to the mining settlement where he was staying. On the following day some forty or fifty of Emery's mates, having made a coffin, set off to carry it to a point near Antler Creek where the dead man had expressed a wish to be buried.

Late in the afternoon, and not far from the burial place, the party met the Bishop and Sheephanks when, said Dundas,

Having first distributed hymn cards to the party, we proceeded, singing the ninetieth psalm, to the spot where the grave was dug. It was on a grassy flat, up a bank by which the trail ran, and some little way in the rear of a settler's log house. Coming in sight of the grave the Bishop read the opening sentences. The friends clustered round; the Bishop, Sheepshanks, and I stood together at the head, . . . Not a few were listening to a preacher for the first time since their childhood! . . . the brother of the deceased stood forward and thanked the Bishop heartily for his great kindness. The attendance of so many of Emery's "mates" was a good instance of the great sympathy and cordiality that exists even among these rough men. Many of them were working for wages, on others' claims . . . but simply to show respect for one whose only connection with them was that he had been a comrade in distress, they were ready to forego a day's work and pay, and take a rough, fatiguing tramp in order to honour his memory. . . .[7]

Not only was the lot of a pioneer missionary a rough one but in order to gain the confidence of his hardened parishioners it was necessary for him to do more than conduct services. Typical of the efforts of such men was the work of the Reverend James Reynard who was ordained by Bishop Hills. He served for a time as Principal of the Indian School in Victoria, and Assistant

Minister at the Cathedral. In the summer of 1867 an appeal was presented from many people of the Cariboo asking for the appointment of a resident priest. Hitherto, one or other of the diocesan clergy had spent a few months each summer in the area. In spite of the opposition of those who felt that he could not possibly survive, and that the Cariboo was no place for a clergyman's wife and family, Reynard and his household moved to Barkerville[8] in August, 1868. He felt that it would be possible to sell a building which had formerly been used as a church, and with the proceeds to build a small cottage. Meanwhile, the services were to be held in a borrowed saloon.

At the first service seats were provided for fifty people and twice that number arrived. The offering was £11·15·od. Reynard wrote enthusiastically to the Bishop:

> Now, I think this very encouraging. Without any appeal or explanation of how I stood dependent on the voluntary offerings of the congregation, I find the offerings averaging half a dollar. More than that, all seemed delighted with the service, and hopeful for the music. The Welsh and the Wesleyans are regretting that their service and the Church service are at the same time as they wish to join with us. Well, they can do so if they wish. I had at both services Jews and Romanists, and Protestant sects of all kinds. Will you kindly send off for me a box of Prayer Books? I am happy to say that all are discontented with the quasi-service and wish the full English Church service . . . . Tomorrow evening I have a public meeting after congregational singing practice, when I shall seek to form a Church Institute Committee to help raise funds for the purchase of the saloon. The owner gives 100 dols., Mr. Walkem 50 dols., the memorialists are ready with their various amounts, and an appeal to the miners will not be unanswered.[9]

For the next few weeks all went well and the missionary's hopes ran high, but by the end of September all hope for the time being had disappeared as the result of a fire which destroyed the whole of the little town leaving the mission without the building they had hoped to sell, without lamps, benches, robes or books. Everything had gone without a trace.

Almost at once work was begun again and Reynard wrote optimistically to the Bishop that there was a great work to be done and that he had made many friends. Not only was he ministering to the people at Barkerville but went as well to Mosquito Creek, Quesnel, Antler, Keithley, Grouse and further still.

The hardships were many—the indifference of those to whom a Christian example was an open challenge, the rigours of a northern winter, the trials of a stipend inadequate to provide proper food and clothing. Unceasing in his efforts to attract the miners to the Church and her services Reynard used his musical talents to form a band which gained the interest of a number of young men. "The band," he wrote, "consists of a clarinet, two flutes, cornet, and bassoon. I preside at the piano. Last night the street was crowded with listeners, and quite a sensation was made; and really we begin to get on very well."[10]

From this he went on to develop a Church Institute. Before the days of motion pictures, radio, and television, the Church Institute was in many places a popular aspect of parish life. Hook established Church popular libraries in Leeds, twenty-eight in all, with reading rooms, open at a subscription of 1d. or 2d. a week.[11] Copied to some extent from the Mechanics' Institutes of the nineteenth century the Church Institute sought to provide education and recreation for all who cared to use its facilities, and on the whole these Institutes had an astonishingly wide and diverse programme.

During the winter of 1869 an ambitious programme was announced for the Barkerville Church Institute. On Monday evenings there would be study of the *Acts of the Apostles* in Greek or English, followed by the reading of Caesar's *De Bello Gallico*. Tuesday evening was occupied by the band practice.

On Wednesday evening the room would be open for reading, study, chess, or similar activity, while on Thursday facilities would be offered for those who wished to study mathematics. Friday was given up to choir practice with an occasional public lecture. The public lecture was another popular feature of the late nineteenth century and anyone who could present an interesting talk, particularly if he could accompany it with lantern slides, was sure of an audience. So the church at Barkerville went on, and although there were those who objected Reynard steadily gained support so that by November, 1869, the church, which still stands, neared completion.

---

1 *Columbia Mission Report*, 1862, p.11.
2 Loc. cit.
3 Quoted from *Speeches delivered by the Lord Bishop of Oxford*, . . . *and other influential friends of the COLUMBIA MISSION, at the Public Meeting in the London Tavern, on Thursday, February 27th*, 1862, p.7. Copy in the Archives of the Ecclesiastical Province of B. C., Vancouver.
4 Howay & Scholefield, *British Columbia*, II, p. 115.
5 *Mission Life*, April, 1868, pp.267-277.
6 Manuscript copy of an article from *Mission Life*, copy in Archives of the Ecclesiastical Province of B.C.
7 *Mission Life*, 1867, pp.154-159.
   This quotation and the preceding one are from manuscript copies of these articles in the Archives, Ecclesiastical Province of B.C.
8 *Columbia Mission Report*, 1868, p.26.
9 *Ibid.*, p.28.
10 *Columbia Mission Report*, 1869, p.55.
11 J. L. and Barbara Hammond, *The Age of the Chartists*, Longmans, Green, London, 1930, p. 327n.

# 5

# Early Stages
# in Organization

ONCE the Bishop had made a preliminary survey of his diocese the next step was to set up some diocesan organization and for this purpose he called a meeting of the pewholders of Christ Church and St. John's Church, Victoria, on Tuesday, January 15th, 1861, a little more than a year after his arrival. Alex A. Dallas was elected to act as chairman and, after speaking of the progress which the Church had already made in the colony for which, he said, thanks were due particularly to Miss Burdett Coutts, he called upon the Bishop to lay before the meeting the proposals he had to make. The Bishop's address included four topics: (1) the present state of the Church in British Columbia; (2) the means of support; (3) questions concerning diocesan and parochial organization; and (4) the possibility of forming a Church Society to function until a diocesan synod could be established.

In discussing the first of these the Bishop was careful to emphasise the fact that the Church in the colony was quite separate from the State, and was in no sense "established."

It may be well to digress briefly to discuss this matter of establishment as it relates to British Columbia. The colony, it will be remembered, had been established by the Hudson's Bay Company in whose hands rested complete control. It had always been the declared policy of the Company, but not always the practice of its servants, to encourage such acts of piety as daily prayers and Sunday services in the various establishments, and where possible the Company appointed chaplains. We have already seen how Beaver and Staines were appointed in this way. Naturally, their connection with the Company itself, and with the Company *qua* government, was a close one. After the establishment of the Crown Colony all appointments of clergy, with the exception of the first Bishop, rested with the Church and there was never any conflict between the Governor and the Bishop as there was in the early days of Nova Scotia and Quebec. It was natural, however, that the Church should look to the colonial government for material help as it had formerly done to the Company. We have already noted requests from Crickmer at Fort Langley and Gammage at Port Douglas for such help.

At the time of the Bishop's arrival Amor de Cosmos, the belligerent editor of the Victoria *Daily British Colonist,* was conducting a vigorous campaign against any sort of State aid to religious bodies, in which he was supported by the militant Dr. W. F. Clarke, the Congregationalist minister in Victoria. This campaign was in part due to the fact that Cridge who had been appointed by the Hudson's Bay Company as Colonial Chaplain for a period of five years had, as the expiry date of his appointment drew near, applied for its renewal not to the Company but to the colonial government which had superseded the Company.

In these circumstances the Bishop was careful to emphasise

the fact that the Church did not look for State support, and in this connection it is worth quoting the Bishop's letter on the subject to the Church Committees at Douglas and Lillooet, both of whom had been promised financial assistance from public funds for their building projects. The Bishop's letter follows:

New Westminster,
July 31st, 1861.

Gentlemen,

I understand grants have been made from the public revenue towards the churches you are building in Douglas and Lillooet.

In what I am about to say, I expose myself to the charge of undue interference since these grants were made, not to me, but to yourselves and your rising towns in aid of your own laudable exertions.

I am sure that the executive has been moved by the highest motives, and a desire to see truth and religion flourish in our land.

I feel, therefore, a great responsibility when I ask you to endeavour to carry on your good work without these grants.
My reasons are:

1. Although given on the fair principle of assisting the first efforts only of a place to build a church, without regard to denomination, there is the certainty of misconstruction, and of the charge of favouritism, causing jealousies and ill-feeling, such as on behalf of the Church of England, which happens in these cases to be "first in the field," I am by all means desirous of preventing.

2. Grants if made at all cannot stop at this point, but must be extended further, and every section of the tax-paying public will have the right to demand a portion of the public money on exactly equal terms, whether for the advancement of truth or error—a result in my opinion embarrassing to a government and not conducive to the glory of God.

3. There exists a wide-spread and deeply rooted objection in the community against such grants; a feeling shared, I believe, almost universally by the Clergy of the Church of England of this Colony.

—Cyril Stackhouse

Derby, 1859, a sketch by the
Reverend W. B. Crickmer showing
how he preached from a barrel
on the main street.

*Reverend John Sheepshanks, missionary at New Westminster.*

Victoria, Nov: 27. 1860.

Sir,

  I have the honor to inform you that I have been enabled to place a clergyman, the Rev: L. L. Brown at Cayoosh. He has been favorably received and the inhabitants have had a meeting at which they have resolved to build a Church.

  I have to request of your Excellency to be so kind as to grant, for the uses of the Church of England, in accordance with former precedents

   a Town Site for Church
       "   "   for Parsonage
   Suburban land for Burial Ground

and the grant, or permission to purchase at the usual price of a five acre Suburban Lot

    I have the honor to be
      Sir,
    Your Excellency' faithful serv.t
       G. Columbia

His Excellency
The Governor

A letter from Bishop Hills dated November 27, 1860.

*Port Douglas at the head of Harrison Lake, about 1862.*

*Nanaimo, about 1862.*

4. The system has been tried in other British possessions, and has either been abandoned as unsuccessful, or is the cause of much irritation and contention, such as we would gladly avoid here.

Should you deem it right to act upon my suggestion and decline all State aid, I am ready, towards the additional burden which must fall upon you, to increase the sum I have already promised from the funds at my disposal, and sincerely trust the good work will still go on.

I am, Gentlemen,

Your faithful friend and Servant,

G. COLUMBIA.[1]

In reply to the Bishop's request the grants were declined and no further such assistance was received.

Even without such aid considerable progress had been made. The number of clergy had increased from one to fifteen, three churches had been built, and services and missionary work were being carried on throughout the two colonies. Two of the parishes, Christ Church, Victoria, and Holy Trinity, New Westminster, were becoming self-supporting, and the Bishop's stipend, together with those for two archdeacons, were provided from the endowments given by Miss Burdett Coutts. The rest of the work in the diocese was being maintained from funds the Bishop had raised in England, from grants from the missionary societies and from a sum of about £1200 a year from pew rents, church collections, school fees and miscellaneous sources.

To return to the January 15th meeting, the Bishop went on to discuss church organization, parochial and diocesan. In England, he said, the parochial organization consisted of the rector, churchwardens, and a vestry made up of all the pewholders. Sometimes there was a select vestry chosen by the general vestry. In the United States the select vestry was found in every parish but known as a Church Committee. For British Columbia he suggested that the parochial organization should consist of the rector, churchwardens, church committee, and vestry. The vestry would consist of all the pewholders who would annually elect a church committee.

It is interesting to note, although the Bishop did not mention it on this occasion, that on August 2nd, 1856, some five years earlier, the Council of Vancouver Island had passed *An Ordinance Establishing Regulations for the Arrangement of the Affairs of the Colonial Church at Victoria*. The colonial church was, of course, Christ Church, and the ordinance provided that the "renters of sittings, being Adults" (pewholders) should hold an annual meeting on the second Wednesday in August each year when they would elect a churchwarden, the other being appointed at the same time by the rector. The main business of the churchwardens was envisaged to be that of appointing "sittings to the people, according to priority of application," making alterations where necessary, and attending to the repairs of the church, "and to such other matters as usually fall to this office in the Church of England." There was no provision for a Church Committee.

Diocesan organization, continued the Bishop, in its complete form consists of an assembly of the bishops, clergy, and lay delegates, meeting annually for deliberation and decision on the many subjects of importance to the welfare of the Church and the success of the Gospel. In nearly all the British Colonies, he pointed out, this organization was now complete but obviously it could not be set up in British Columbia until parochial organization was further advanced. In the interim he suggested the formation of a Church Society.

A Church Society consisted of subscribers throughout the diocese who were incorporated for holding property and administering it, building churches, supporting clergy and lay workers and making provision for widows and orphans of clergy. The income of such a society came from church collections and individual subscriptions and was administered by a committee chosen from the subscribers. The particular example the Bishop took to illustrate his point was the Toronto Church Society which now, he said, had an annual income of £9,000. At the close of the meeting a number of resolutions were passed to effect the Bishop's suggestions.

Even when such assistance had been provided the Bishop quickly realised the utter impossibility of providing adequate episcopal oversight for the vast area which had been committed to him, and soon began to speak in terms of dividing the diocese. The case for an additional bishop was strengthened by the fact that in the year preceding Hills' consecration a separate civil administration, the Crown Colony of British Columbia, had been set up for the mainland as distinct from Vancouver Island. As early as 1862 the Bishop wrote in the *Columbia Mission Report*

> I propose to bring this [matter of the division of the diocese] before the notice of those in authority, whose approval will be necessary before any step can be taken. The Bishop should be able personally to visit, each year, every Cure in his Diocese. There are places to which I have never yet been able to go. The increased area of mining ground, and the enterprise and excitement that exist for a considerable period of the year in the upper country, demand the close attention of the Bishop. To give this and visit other portions of the Diocese is impossible. My opinion is, the Diocese should be divided into three, and at no distant day, into four.[2]

The Bishop visited England in 1863 and pressed his point of view with the result that in July of the following year the Colonial Bishoprics Council recorded its conviction of the "importance of separating Vancouver's Island from the Diocese of British Columbia, and erecting it into a separate Bishopric as soon as the necessary fund for its endowment can be provided."[3] While the Bishop was convinced of the necessity for division he seems to have been uncertain of the way in which it should be carried out. At one point he argued that the boundary should be the natural watershed between the Fraser and the Pacific so that Vancouver Island, the coastal islands, and the lower mainland would all remain in the diocese of British Columbia, leaving the interior for the new bishop. While this view was, for a time at least, supported by the Archbishop of Canterbury and the Colonial Bishoprics Council, it was opposed by the Colonial Office. The decision was then made to make the new dioceses coterminous with the two existing crown colonies.

On the strength of this decision an appeal[4] was launched for the Diocese of New Westminster, and signed by John Postlethwaite as Bishop-designate. Who Postlethwaite was, or by whom he was nominated, is not clear, but in July, 1866, Bishop Hills wrote to the S.P.G.[5] expressing anticipation of his forthcoming consecration and arrival, but there the matter ended and nothing more was heard of Postlethwaite. Nor was anything further done about the division of the diocese for some years. It is possible that when Postlethwaite's consecration did not materialize it was considered wise not to proceed with the division since the colonies which had been united under one government in 1866 were "suffering from a disastrous commercial depression, affecting all interests."[6]

During the next few years events were taking place in Victoria and in the northern part of the diocese which were to have a pronounced effect upon the division when it did take place. It will be remembered that in 1855 the Hudson's Bay Company had brought the Reverend Edward Cridge to Victoria, whom the Bishop later appointed Dean. In the following year the C.M.S. sent William Duncan as a lay catechist to the Tsimshian Indians at Fort Simpson. Both men were militant Evangelicals, not a little unorthodox in their views, and both ultimately left the Church. In 1872-74 Dean Cridge had a disagreement with the Bishop which will be discussed later. Its immediate consequence was that Duncan, who was a close friend of Cridge, hearing that the Bishop intended to visit him, sent word that he should make peace with his brother in Victoria before he presumed to come as a missionary to the Indians. Bishop Hills realised that in the circumstances it would do little good for him to insist on making the visit, and he therefore arranged that Bishop Bompas of Atha- basca, himself a C.M.S. missionary like Duncan, should carry out the visitation.

Bishop Hills also realised that there would be small chance of peace while Duncan remained in his diocese and so, while in England in 1879, brought forward a new suggestion that the diocese should be divided into three. Bishop Hills would retain Vancouver Island with the original title of British Columbia; the lower mainland would become the diocese of New West- minster; and the northern part of the province could be consti- tuted as the diocese of Caledonia. The scheme was accepted and the C.M.S. whose mission fields comprised the only work being done in the new diocese of Caledonia, agreed to nominate the bishop and to provide his stipend. Their choice fell upon the Reverend William Ridley, formerly a missionary in India, and at that time Vicar of St. Paul's, Huddersfield. He was consecrated on St. James' Day, July 25th, 1879. New Westminster was to continue in the tradition of the S.P.G., and that society was invited to nominate the first bishop. The S.P.G. put forth the name of the Reverend Acton Windeyer Sillitoe, M.A., (Can- tab.), then chaplain at Darmstadt, who was consecrated in Croy- don Parish Church on All Saints' Day, 1879. To these two bishops and their work we shall return, but our immediate task must be to watch the progress of the now reduced diocese of British Columbia.

We have already seen the concern of Bishop Hills to set up a measure of diocesan organization. In this he had been encouraged and even urged to proceed by the S.P.G., and opposed, although on the flimsiest grounds, by Dean Cridge and his friends who are sometimes described as the family-company-compact. Reference has already been made to the setting up of the Church Society but thereafter the Bishop explained that he was waiting for the division of the diocese before proceeding further. When it became apparent that the division was likely to be delayed, he summoned a meeting in Victoria on September 24th, 1868. After surveying the progress of the diocese since its inception the Bishop pointed out that support from England was declining and that measures had to be taken towards self-support. He felt that the time was not yet ripe for the organization of a regular Diocesan Synod but that the needs of the situation might be met by the more active participation of the Diocesan Church Society. This met with general agreement and a committee was established to set up a general fund in support of the work of the Church in the Colony. A year later, when its annual meeting was held, it was generally felt that a great deal had been accomplished, and that the Society was fully justifying the hopes and expectations of its supporters.

The real and ultimate need, however, was for a fully organized diocesan synod, and in December, 1873, the matter was discussed by the committee of the diocesan Church Society. With the assent of that committee the Bishop invited various church committees to meet with him in January of the new year. He also preached a sermon on "Synods, their Constitution and Objects," in Christ Church and St. John's, Victoria. At the meeting of the church committees resolutions were passed accepting the idea of a synod and recommending an election of delegates to take place at Easter. Further meetings were held and a provisional executive committee was set up, and the first session of the new Synod held almost two years later in December, 1875. The delay in summoning it may well have been due to the unfortunate Cridge affair, and perhaps because of this the Bishop was careful, in his introductory address, to deal with all the possible objections. The synod, however, was fairly launched and became an accepted part of diocesan machinery, with regular meetings, although it was not incorporated by Act of the Provincial Legislature until 1889.

The early meetings of the synod were all concerned with the routine matters connected with diocesan life, such as the adoption of canons, provision of pension funds, and the building of churches, parsonages, and schools. Before long finance became an increasing problem. Gifts in England to the Columbia Mission Fund decreased, and the S.P.G. felt it necessary to curtail its grants to the diocese, suspending them altogether in 1882. As a result of this lessened income it was felt that it might be necessary to abandon several missions.[7]

The next few years constituted a period of extreme difficulty. Stipends were not always paid in full and it would appear that most of the Indian work was allowed to lapse. By 1892 it was reported that the only Indian worker in the diocese was that at Alert Bay supported by the C.M.S., and schools at Nanaimo and on the Songhees Reserve maintained by the Indian Department but supported by friends of the Church. What was done depended largely upon the energy and personal generosity of the Bishop, and his success in raising funds in England. These were supplemented by the S.P.C.K. and by the work of a group of ladies associated with Mrs. Hills. During this period, in spite of financial stringency, new churches and missions were opened up and the work of the Church, among white settlers at least, was expanded.

At the synod of 1888 the Bishop intimated that he felt the time had come when he should resign the see and relinquish the work to a younger man. Although he did not say so at the time it was known that he was also concerned about the health of Mrs. Hills and wished to take her to England where she might spend her last days in more peaceful surroundings. Within a few weeks, however, she had died and the Bishop decided to remain at his post for the time being. By 1892 failing strength warned him that his active days were over and he resigned the see, returning to England where he spent his last few years in a quiet country parish in the Diocese of Norwich.

There was some difficulty in electing a successor and the matter was referred to the Archbishop of Canterbury who nominated the Reverend William Wilcox Perrin, M.A., Vicar of St. Luke's, Southampton.

He was consecrated in Westminster Abbey on March 25th, 1893, in company with the Reverend W. J. Burn, Bishop-designate of Qu'Appelle. Bishop Perrin arrived in his diocese about two months later and was enthroned at a public service on June 29th, the day of his first Synod. His episcopate was relatively short and uneventful, and in 1911 he became the first Suffragan Bishop of Willesden. Looking back over his years in British Columbia just before he left he was able to report that the diocese was practically self-supporting and that the prospects for the future were bright.[8] The situation of the Indians left much to be desired and they needed both guidance and protection.

Bishop Perrin was succeeded by the Right Reverend John Charles Roper, who was consecrated in 1912, and translated to Ottawa three years later. His successor, the Right Reverend Augustine Scriven, who had been Archdeacon of Vancouver

(Island) since 1884, lived a bare nine months after his consecration and was succeeded by the Right Reverend Charles DeVeber Schofield.

Bishop Schofield[9] had been invited to succeed Archdeacon Pentreath at the time of the latter's death but felt constrained to decline and later became Dean of Fredericton. From thence he was brought by Bishop Roper to become Dean of Columbia, only to be elected bishop a year or so later when Dr. Roper moved to Ottawa. The twenty years of his episcopate were indeed difficult for they began during the first Great War and continued through the time of reconstruction. Perhaps the most obvious, though not necessarily the most important, accomplishment of his episcopate was the construction of the Memorial Hall and the building and opening of the great stone nave of the new Cathedral, the former in 1924, and the latter five years later. During the next few years Bishop Schofield's health was failing and in 1935 he asked for the election of a coadjutor-bishop. The Reverend Harold Eustace Sexton was elected, and a little more than a year later the bishop was dead.

---

1 *Columbia Mission Report*, 1861, p.34.

2 *Columbia Mission Report*, 1862, p.7.

3 *Columbia Mission Report*, 1863, p.6.

4 *Columbia Mission Report*, 1866, p.9.

5 Letter from Bishop Hills to the S.P.G., July 7, 1866. Microfilm of transcript of letter in Archives of the Ecclesiastical Province of B. C.

6 *Columbia Mission Report*, 1867, p.7.

7 Proceedings, Synod of the Diocese of British Columbia, October, 1881, p.9ff.

8 *Year Book*, British Columbia Church Aid Society, 1911, pp. 37-8.

9 *Charles DeVeber Schofield, Late Bishop of British Columbia*, by Emily M. Schofield, his wife, published privately, Victoria, 1941.

# The Church
# and Education

MISSIONARY activity in the Pacific northwest began, as we have seen, with the appointment of schoolmaster-chaplains by the Hudson's Bay Company: Herbert Beaver at Fort Vancouver and then Robert John Staines at Victoria. With the death of Staines and the establishment of the Crown Colony of Vancouver Island at almost the same time, the active participation of the Company in educational affairs came to an end.

However, in spite of the official separation of Company and government, there still remained a close connection for James Douglas continued to stand at the head of both. In his capacity as Governor of the Crown Colony he did much for the establishment of the Common Schools, the first at Victoria in 1852, and others at Nanaimo and Craigflower the following year. For these the Church was in no way responsible so that public secular education was early established in British Columbia. At the same time, it is worth noting that the secular schools were not intended to be irreligious for the Scriptures were taught in them.[1]

The third chaplain of the Hudson's Bay Company at Victoria was the Reverend Edward Cridge, whom we have already met. Whatever his weaknesses in other directions Cridge was eminently public-spirited and did much for the cause of education in the colony. For a time he served as Superintendent of Education under the colonial government. It was not intended that he should maintain a school as his predecessors had done but at the time of his appointment the Governor of the Company in London wrote to Douglas saying, "The Company think it very desirable that the Clergyman should as is done at Red River by the Bishop of Rupert's Land take charge of a Boarding School of a superior class for the children of their officers and would wish that he should take out with him a gentleman and his wife capable of keeping a school of this nature."[2] Cridge did not bring a schoolmaster with him but his wife opened a private school similar to that which had been maintained by Mrs. Staines. Thus were sown the seeds of the future Church schools of British Columbia to which we shall turn later.

We may turn first to the mission schools established among the Indians. It seems probable that the first attempt to instruct the Indians of Vancouver Island in the Christian faith was undertaken by a Roman Catholic priest in 1849 or 1850, although there had been visits by Roman clergy before that. The Oblate historian Morice says that when Bishop Modeste Demers came to Victoria to take possession of his diocese in 1851 he discovered that "one had been there whom he cordially wished had never left his native country. . . . That ill-advised missionary had lived nine months in the midst of the Cowichan tribe, but he had taken his departure prior to the bishop coming to take possession of his see."[3] O'Hara adds that when Demers arrived "he was lodged in a little house which had been built by the Hudson's Bay Company for the use of Father Lamfrit, o.m.i., who had been sent to

Victoria early in March, 1849."[4] It is natural enough that Morice would not wish to reveal the identity of his colleague, whose work was so unsuccessful and who certainly cannot be said to have established a school.

Reference has already been made to the fact that Dowson, the first missionary of the S.P.G. to the new Diocese of British Columbia, settled down to work among the Indians at Craigflower but stayed only a short time. No one was available to replace him at once but in April, 1860, the Reverend Alexander C. Garrett, B.A., (Trinity College, Dublin), arrived with his wife and two children. Shortly afterwards he entered upon his duties as missionary to the Indians. In his reminiscences[5] he described Victoria as being a town of some three thousand people and said that across the harbour there was an Indian reservation with a population of about two thousand. Shortly before his arrival there had been an incident when some Indians had fired upon a British schooner and a show of force had been used to arrest and punish the delinquents. Garrett, learning of this, appealed to the Bishop for permission to open a school amongst them, only to be told that he had not been brought from England to minister to these natives, and that in any case there were no funds available. The missionary, nothing daunted, volunteered to use a bell tent which he had brought from England. With the help of some men from H.M.S. *Satellite* he set it up with a wooden floor, and built some rough and ready desks. The school opened with 54 pupils speaking five different languages. The difficulty of teaching them can be imagined but was overcome at least temporarily by the use of the Chinook jargon which was known to all of them.

The work continued for a year or more until one bright morning when the missionary appeared only the ribs of the tent were to be seen. Shortly afterwards a fleet of canoes came in sight with new canvas sails spread out to the breeze! There were those who

ESQUIMALT CHURCH, BRITISH COLUMBIA.—*From a Photograph.*

*From an engraving in the Columbia Mission Report, 1868*

argued that such results might be expected, and that any effort among the Indians was doomed to failure. The missionary and his friends persisted in spite of discouragement and the sum of one thousand dollars was raised in Victoria to build a wooden house on the reservation to replace the vanished tent. This house was "built in the shape of an octagon, so that one division might be used by the Missionary, while the children of the several tribes who did not love each other might be placed in the others. A small dwelling was also erected into which the Missionary moved his little family."[6]

Garrett continued his reminiscences by saying that "his duties were now to ride on Sunday mornings into the country to a little Mission about fifteen miles away; return to the Indian school for the afternoon service, and occupy the pulpit in Christ Church Cathedral as evening lecturer. This happy combination of physical, mental, and ministerial work," he said, "kept me in good health and cheerful spirits."[7]

After a year or so the Reverend John Booth Good, a recent graduate of St. Augustine's College, Canterbury, arrived with his wife to take up work in the diocese and was assigned by the Bishop to assist Garrett in the Victoria Indian Mission. This seems to have been but a temporary expedient until the best means of using his services could be decided, and in September, 1861, he was appointed to the newly established parish of St. Paul, Nanaimo.

As Good had been trained as a schoolmaster, and had actually taught in a Lincolnshire village school for three years, it might have been supposed that he would take an active personal interest in the work of the Indian school there to be established. This was not the case, however, and beyond describing how the church and school were built he seems to have been content to turn over the educational work to a catechist, Jordayne C. B.

Cave, who was appointed to assist him. Good did remark that the Methodists had been working among the Indians for some time and had established a school. They therefore viewed the new Anglican Mission as something of an intrusion. Cornelius Bryant had opened a school in the Methodist cause in 1857, and the Reverend Arthur Browning, a minister of that denomination, arrived at Nanaimo early in 1859.

Cave's first impressions were not encouraging. He opened the school on December 1st, 1862, when nine very dirty and untidy children presented themselves. His first task was to assure them of the need for cleanliness, apparently with good results for he remarked that when he sent three of them home to wash a few days later they regarded themselves as having been disgraced in the eyes of their fellows. Little more is reported from Nanaimo though it would seem that satisfactory progress was made and that each week Good came in to examine and catechise the children.

Meanwhile, Garrett, at the Victoria Indian Mission, had begun to travel further afield, visiting other Indian tribes and holding services among them. One of these centres was Cowichan where his work was hindered by the Roman Catholic missionaries who, shortly after he began to hold services there, stationed a resident priest among the natives, and a much more competent priest, apparently, than the inexperienced young man who had first visited them in the Roman cause. In 1866 the Bishop was able to appoint the Reverend W. S. Reece, M.A., as resident missionary to the twelve hundred Indians in the vicinity, and shortly afterwards W. Henry Lomas was added to the staff as a catechist. Upon him fell the responsibility for the maintenance of the school.

A school chapel, with catechist's residence, was erected and the work of the school began in the summer of 1867. At first the children's attendances were quite irregular, the more so since they came with neither encouragement nor hindrance from their parents. In June, 1867, the catechist reported that

> All seemed very pleased at the idea of a school being opened, and the Quamachan chief [Tee-che-mult] offered the use of a small log cabin in which to hold the school until the Chapel was completed; others promised to clean out the building; and the next morning a school was opened for the boys at which eighteen attended. All appeared eager to learn. Of course, the instruction was of a very elementary nature, and I fear we can have but little hope of imparting much religious instruction until the language has been acquired. The school was kept open for a fortnight, with an average attendance of twelve; but at the end of that time all the boys left the village to go with their families to different stations on the coast to fish for clams, and gather roots that grow on the hillsides, which they dry for winter use. This will, for some time, be one drawback of the work of teaching the young as at intervals, throughout the summer, they all go away to fish, etc., but this will, I think, be lessened as each family clears ground, and fences in gardens which they will not like to leave. A few did this last winter, and they have not left their houses this summer as formerly. Some few have cattle of their own, and one man has already had a "bee" to build a barn, at which both white men and natives assisted.[8]

One of the first Indian schools to be established in the Northwest was the one at Fort Simpson by William Duncan whom we have already met. Here we are concerned only with the work of his school. Soon after Duncan's arrival in 1858, Legaic, the head chief, offered his house for use as a school and on the morning of its opening some twenty-six children appeared, followed by fifteen adults in the afternoon.[9] Later in the summer, with the assistance of the Indians, a building was erected for the purpose and equipped with desks and benches. When the new school was opened on November 17th, all the former scholars were present together with many more, so that in all there were 140 children and 50 adults.

A larger building was erected soon afterwards but Duncan

had already come to his conclusion that a Christian Indian village could only be established beyond the reach of depraved and demoralising whites. To this end, as we have seen already, he established his new colony at Metlakatla.

The large schoolhouse, which had been built with its removal in view, was taken down, put on a raft, and floated to its new site. We may believe that the work of education was begun again almost at once and that the curriculum although practical was coloured by Duncan's peculiar theological views. It is interesting to note that the accounts of visits to Metlakatla by the Bishop and others in the *Columbia Mission Reports* are much longer than those of any similar visits, and all contain detailed reports of the examination of candidates for baptism in some such form as this:

| Name | Age | Answers |
|---|---|---|
| LEGAIC . . . (Principal Chief) | 40 | We must put away all our evil ways. I want to take hold of God. I believe in God the Father who made all things, and in Jesus Christ. I constantly cry for my sins when I remember them. I believe the good will sit near God after death. Am anxious to walk in God's ways all my life. . . . |
| QU·TL·NOH . . . | 19 | I wish to put away all sin, lies, drunkenness. Have erred in following man. Must now try to follow God. I believe in Jesus Christ, who died for our sin. God's spirit prepares us for baptism. We shall rise from the dead and see God's face, if we are God's children. I am wishful to serve God as long as I live. |

SHOODAHSL . . . 30
(Wife of Clah)

We must give up all sin. God sees and knows us all through. Jesus died in our state [*sic*] because we were bad. By the Spirit of Jesus we must learn to walk in the good way. I feel struggle in my mind but persevere. I pray for pardon. Will do all I can to keep God's way. God's own Word promises that he will hear.[10]

On the mainland one of the earliest schools for Indians seems to have been the one established at Lytton by the Reverend John Good. In 1866 Good had volunteered his services for work on the mainland and had, with the consent of the Bishop, moved to Yale as a temporary centre. He had not been there long when his attention was drawn to the spiritual needs and interest of the Thompson Indians around Lytton, many of whom had received a superficial introduction to the Christian Faith from the Roman Catholic clergy who had passed through at an earlier date. In March of the following year, a large body of the Lytton Indians came as a deputation to Yale to take part in the Sunday worship and to make request for a missionary to come to them. Were such provided they could, they said, promise a huge gathering of Indians of their tribe. Good promised to lay the matter before the Bishop. At the end of April he received a further urgent request from Lytton in the form of a telegram in the Chinook jargon, which read, *"Lytton siwashes tum tum mika cloosh hyaek chaco. Tikke wawwa mika"* (the Lytton Indians think you had better make haste and come. They wish to speak to you).[11]

Feeling that he had no alternative, and encouraged by the knowledge that David Holmes, a young ordinand, would be arriving to assist at Yale within a few days, Good set out for Lytton where he was met by five hundred Indians who urged him to come and live among them. So great was their insistence that he felt that with the Bishop's permission, he ought to accede to their request. He therefore conducted the services at Yale on June 9th, 1867, preaching from Exodus 33.15, and in the following week moved with his family to Lytton. There, on June 16th, he held a service for the Indians in a building formerly used as a store but which had been lent to the Church until other arrangements could be made. "About two hundred," Good reported, "were present, and our red cross banner floated over as we, the heralds of the Cross of Jesus, sought to speak unto this interesting people 'all the words of this life'."[12]

At the end of August he opened the Indian Boys' School when

> four cleanly lads, with intelligent countenances, . . . presented themselves . . . for consecutive religious and secular instruction and training. My first day's intercourse with them and trial of their qualities show me that they are capable of a rapid and high development. At 10 a.m. the flag goes up, and the bell is rung for prayers. Then to work until 12, followed by an hour's recess when the flag is half-mast. At 1 resume school; conclude at 3 p.m. Industrial work from 3 to 4, and occasional evening classes. All the boys are expected to attend both the native and white services on the Sunday. I give them a little drill every day to enliven them up, and impart habits of instant obedience, etc., whilst their hours of play are sufficiently long to prevent them feeling the hours of work irksome and confining.[13]

As the year went on the attendance increased and Good evidently looked forward to the establishment of a residential school for he said that those already enrolled would

> form the nucleus of our Indian Training Institution for both sexes. It is not easy to induce parents to give up their boys this year to attend school continuously, and to provide them with food as boarders, as also to help with their clothing, owing to the great dearth of salmon and berries, which makes all very apprehensive of suffering to come when the winter sets in . . .[14]

The boarding school did not materialise and it even seems doubtful whether a day school building was erected. The work of teaching was carried on in the Mission House and Indian church. Moreover, as we have already seen, Good did not feel able to devote his whole time to the work of the school. After Archdeacon Woods had visited Lytton in the summer of 1869 he reported that

> Mr. Good finds it difficult to carry on the school regularly, owing to the calls on his time for visiting distant tribes, which visits take time away from Lytton sometimes for a month at a time . . . . It will then be seen that to work this mission efficiently it requires: 1. a suit-able site for the industrial training school; 2. an assistant who will either take some of the outlying districts off Mr. Good's hands, or, working with him in Lytton, will enable him to visit outlying districts without interrupting the work.[15]

In 1884 the Reverend John Good returned to Nanaimo and was succeeded by the Reverend Richard Small, M.A. (Cantab.) who came to British Columbia from England to undertake the work at the invitation of Bishop Sillitoe. In 1897 he became superintendent of all the Indian Missions in the diocese with the title of Archdeacon of Yale. In a very real sense he became the apostle to the Thompson River Indians ministering to them lovingly and unceasingly until his death in 1909.

Brought up in a strongly Evangelical atmosphere, Archdeacon Small absorbed much of the Catholic or Tractarian tradition, not through mere imitation but from a conviction born of constant and continuing study of the Tractarian leaders and the Early Fathers of the Church. Indeed, it is said that the extraordinary weight of his travelling bag was due to the fact that he always carried a volume or two of patristic theology with him.

At the time of his death it was written of him that no pains were too great, no journeys too arduous, no sacrifice too costly to win the Indians to the Gospel of Christ. He followed them in their migrations, lived with them in their houses, and even in the curious underground pits in which they sheltered themselves from the bitter winter's cold—instructing them, preparing them for their Communions at the Great Festivals, hearing their complaints, settling their disputes, promoting their interests, and identifying himself with them in every way. The distances he covered were enormous—the northern Cariboo settlements, and Nicola, Lillooet, Yale, Chilliwack—he visited them all in turn, taking much pleasure in his work. His last visit to England he cut short to be back in time to prepare his Indians for their Christmas Communion. Arriving in Lytton, he wrote, "what a happiness it is to be back again with the Indians in their Church."[16]

The boarding school which Good had foreseen came into being in 1901 with the aid of the New England Company, a society which, it should be explained, was "England's first organised effort for the propagation of the Gospel amongst the heathen, and was the outcome of the early suggestions of some clergy of the Church of England and other Ministers of the Gospel, made some years before but which did not bear fruit until the year A.D. 1649, when, at the instance of Oliver Cromwell and others, an Ordinance was passed by the Long Parliament which created the Company 'for promoting and propagating the Gospel of Jesus Christ (amongst the Indians) in New England'."[17] Thirty years before the New England Company had made grants of £50 each towards the salaries of teachers in the Indian schools at Cowichan and Lytton. Now its clerk wrote again to know how the Company could assist in extending work among the Indians, and the Bishop of New Westminster (Dart) replied stating the need for an Industrial School. Negotiations were speedily completed and the school, known as St. George's, was opened on June 7th, 1901, with the Reverend George Ditcham as Principal.[18]

Other day schools in connection with the Indian missions were set up at Alberni and Yale. At Alberni the missionary was the Reverend J. X. Willemar, a former Roman Catholic priest who had been a teacher at the St. Louis College in Victoria. After his reception into the Anglican Communion by Bishop Hills, he arrived at Alberni in July, 1868, having with him Henry Guillod who was to act as lay catechist. Guillod assumed responsibility for the school and expressed some disappointment that his efforts were not more immediately successful. He opened the school in August

> with fourteen boys who came with washed hands and faces, quiet and attentive. Several adults were present, and seemed much interested, especially in the pictures by the aid of which I was explaining the Creation, Deluge, etc.! Those who knew any Chinook or English were helping me with the others. Afterwards I was much disappointed in the school—those who attended regularly having learnt the alphabet and to write letters on the slate and the English names of things, etc., when some Indians from Ewkloolaht [Ucluelet] told them that the boys who came to school whose names we wrote down would die; the children got frightened, and I could not persuade them to continue their attendance.[19]

At Yale, David Holmes who had just arrived from St. Augustine's College, Canterbury, came to assist the Reverend John Good in May, 1867. A plan had been drawn up for the erection of a schoolroom at Yale but owing to lack of funds the buildings had been postponed. Holmes, however, felt the importance of a school and began operations in the parsonage. The Bishop sent him twenty dollars' worth of supplies and with these, a few benches, and the back of a tray for a blackboard, he went to work. On the first morning eight boys appeared. Within a few weeks he was glad to report that the enrollment had grown to twenty-one boys and nine girls. He was also conducting a Sunday School with an average attendance of twenty-three.

At Yale, too, about this time occurred one of the not infrequent acts of interference by the Roman Catholic missionaries. In 1861 a member of the Oblate order was stationed at Fort Hope and thenceforward their missionaries were active in the area baptizing the children indiscriminately wherever they could find them. On one occasion as the children were going from school, said Holmes, "the Romish priest was waiting for them, called them into his house, and tried to extort a promise that they would not come to school again. 'If they came, they would go to Hell.' This the children told me, and were encouraged still to come."[20]

In the earliest days of missionary work, and to some extent still, it was necessary to provide not only church and schools for the Indians but also some of the services which now are provided by medical and social agencies. To counteract the baleful influence of the pagan medicine men Dr. Arthur Pearse was appointed Missionary Doctor in 1888,[21] but his work was hindered by the ignorance and naivete of the Indians themselves. If, for example, he prescribed pills to be taken one or two each day the Indians would reason that if one or two daily would do them good, why not take all at once and be cured quickly. It was partly for this reason that St. Bartholomew's Indian Hospital was built at Lytton and opened on August 26th, 1893, by the Bishop. Sister Frances from St. Luke's Home, Vancouver, was the matron.[22] The first hospital was burned down some years afterwards and replaced by the present building. A second hospital was operated for a time at Shulus.

We turn now to the provision made for white children in the diocese. One of Bishop Hills' first concerns on arrival in his new diocese was to see adequate provision made for the secondary education of sons and daughters of Church families. In establishing such schools he felt not only that an immediate need would be met but that the seeds would be planted of "a germ of sound Religious learning, which might be hereafter the great Northern University of these western regions; and which might send forth Missionaries onwards to lighten even China itself."[23]

To this end the Bishop was able to secure the services of the Reverend Charles Thomas Woods, M.A. (Trinity College, Dublin), as Principal of the Boys' Collegiate School, together with those of the Reverend Octavius Glover, M.A., (Cantab.), a priest of distinguished scholarship and ample private means who willingly gave himself to the same work. In Mrs. C. T. Woods he found an able Principal of the "Female Institution" as it was first called. With her were Catherine and Anna Penrice who for ten years had served as District Visitors under Bishop Hills when he was Vicar of Great Yarmouth, and who were now supported in their work by Miss Burdett Coutts. A new brick building on Victoria's Burdett Avenue, still standing but now a private hotel, was opened in 1866 to house Angela College.

The Reverend John Good, in his reminiscences, has left an amusing sidelight on the Penrice sisters who, he says,

> were noted for their personal piety and love for the Church service, and were always conspicuous by their presence and garb [in Church]. But with all their intense anxiety to be exemplary and to profit by what they heard, the sweet, dulcet voice of the Rector [Cridge] gradually closed their eyes and sank them into forgetfulness. On returning to their quarters, these good and holy women regularly sat on the stool of penitence and had their bad half hour. 'Oh, Annie,' was the plaintive cry of sister Sophia, [*sic*] the elder, 'what shall we do? Asleep again during the sermon in spite of all our resolves and self-reproaches to the contrary.'[24]

The day school at Yale was, unfortunately, allowed to lapse, partly through lack of men, and partly through lack of funds to support them. It is sad to think of how much Indian work in British Columbia has suffered in this way. In 1884, however, the Indians of Yale made application to the Church for the establishment of a school for their children, pledging in support some moneys owing to them for their work in railway construction. The school was opened in February, 1884 in a "fairly large house belonging to Mr. Oppenheimer"[25] in Yale under the direction of the Reverend E. L. Wright, the resident missionary.

Later in the year the Bishop was able to enlist the aid of the Community of All Hallows', Ditchingham, Norfolk, who sent Sister Elizabeth, Sister Amy, and Sister Alice to organize an Indian girls' school. They began their work in the Mission House but in May, 1888, took over the former residence of Andrew Onderdonk, one of the contractors in the construction of the Canadian Pacific Railway.[26] This building, with some alterations, afforded much more commodious quarters and Archdeacon Woods, after visiting the school in the summer of that year, wrote to the Sister in charge,

> Allow me . . . to offer my congratulations on the great advantages which must attend on the change from the old premises to the new—from the cramped and confined old parsonage to the roomy, well-built house and extensive grounds of Brookside, affording, as it does, not merely better and more spacious sitting rooms, dormitories, and school room, bath room and a never-failing supply of water but what I consider a special advantage to a girls' school, that you are now a little outside of the town, and have ample space within your own fence for exercise and recreation.[27]

A few years later the school was extended by the erection of an additional building at a cost of $3,500, towards which the Dominion Government made a grant of $1,500. The Government also contributed $60 per annum towards the maintenance of each Indian pupil—about half the actual cost—and there was a small grant from the Society for the Promotion of Christian Knowledge. The enlargement of the school also made it possible for the Sisters to receive a few white boarders,[28] and later on the

73

work of the school was divided into two branches, the Indian School and the Canadian School, which was the name somewhat oddly chosen to describe the department for white children. By 1898, the enrollment had risen to 36 Indian, and 20 white, girls; and many more would have come had there been sufficient accommodation.

The school continued its work for several more years until conditions imposed by the Great War made it necessary to close the Canadian School in September, 1915.[29] This placed the Indian School in a very precarious position, and the New England Company generously offered to transfer it to Lytton where it would be near St. George's School for Boys. This move was brought about some years later, the remaining Sisters returned to England, and All Hallows' Indian Girls' School amalgamated with St. George's School.

---

1 The story of public education in British Columbia is told in an unpublished Ph.D. Thesis by D. L. McLaurin. Copy in the library of the University of British Columbia.

2 Quoted by D. L. McLaurin, op. cit., p.21.

3 A. G. Morice, O.M.I. *History of the Catholic Church in Western Canada*, Musson, Toronto, 1910, II, pp. 297-8.

4 Edwin V. O'Hara, *Catholic History of Oregon*, Catholic Book Co., Portland, 1925, 3rd. Edn, p.116.

5 Typescript copy in the Archives of the Ecclesiastical Province of British Columbia, Vancouver, B. C.

6 *Ibid.*

7 *Ibid.*

8 *Columbia Mission Report*, 1867, p. 38.

9 J. W. Arctander, *The Apostle of Alaska*, Fleming H. Revell, New York, 1909, p.126.

10 *Columbia Mission Report*, 1863, pp.28, 31, and 32.

11 *Columbia Mission Report*, 1867, p.76.

12 *Ibid.*, p.78.

13 *Ibid.*, p.80.

14 *Ibid.*, p.81.

15 *Columbia Mission Report*, 1869, p. 32.

16 *Work for The Far West*, July 1909, p.10.

17 C. Augustus Webb, *The New England Company: A Short History*, 1921.
18 From an unpublished essay by A. R. Hives, The Anglican Theological College, Vancouver, B. C.
19 *Columbia Mission Report*, 1868, p.22.
20 *Columbia Mission Report*, 1869, p.36.
21 *Churchman's Gazette*, Vol. VIII, No. 8, Nov., 1888, p.561
22 *Churchman's Gazette*, Vol. XIII, No. 6, Oct., 1893.
23 *Columbia Mission Report*, 1860, p.14.
24 *The Utmost Bounds of the West*, unpublished manuscript by the Reverend J. B. Good, Provincial Archives, Victoria, B. C.
25 *Churchman's Gazette*, Vol. III, No. 12, March, 1884, p. 331.
26 *Inland Sentinel*, April 7th, 1888.
27 *Churchman's Gazette*, Vol. VIII, No. 5, Aug., 1888, p. 539.
28 *Churchman's Gazette*, Vol. X, No. 11, Feb., 1891, p. 794.
29 Journal of the 34th Session of the Synod of the Diocese of New Westminster, May 8th and 9th, 1917, p.59.

*Angela College, Victoria, from an engraving in*
*Columbia Mission Report, 1868*

# 7

# The Cridge
# Controversy

ANGLICANISM in British Columbia has not been free of tensions—but then Anglicanism is never free of tension and this is not necessarily a bad thing. Those most obvious in Church life in this Province have concerned the inter-relationships of Church and State, and the rather less pleasant internal difficulties of churchmanship. Both, however, are not matters peculiar to this province but are part of the wider picture. Differences between Church and State were largely resolved by the extraordinary foresight of George Hills, the first bishop, in advising congregations not to accept the financial assistance which had been willingly extended from the public purse by the Governor, James Douglas.

Internal tensions were far less happily resolved and in the instance before us the ultimate resolution has still to take place more than three-quarters of a century afterwards. The incidents which led to the suspension of the Very Reverend Edward

Cridge from his office as Dean of Columbia and Rector of Christ Church, Victoria, and the subsequent formation of the Church of our Lord under the auspices of the Reformed Episcopal body may have been due, in small part, to a clash of personalities but it was far more than a local incident. It was, in fact, the local expression of tensions which were being felt throughout the Anglican Communion.

In 17th century England the Church settled down to become the comfortable Department of State, little more than the guardian of public morals, and not always too searching a guardian at that. In direct opposition to this easy-going Latitudinarianism came the Methodist revival at the beginning of the 18th century which through the preaching of the brothers John and Charles Wesley and others emphasised the need for conversion from sin, personal religious life, and the free approach of the individual to his Creator without the mediation of Church or priest. It is not a matter of credit to the Established Church that the Methodists came to feel that they could not remain within her communion. At the end of the 18th century there occurred the Evangelical Revival within the Church with virtually the same objectives. This revival resulted in the foundation of the Church Missionary Society in 1799 and the Colonial and Continental Church Society in 1838. The former was concerned primarily, if not entirely, with ministrations to the heathen, and the latter with providing a ministry to those who had left the church of their fathers to settle in distant lands. It was to this school of thought that Edward Cridge belonged, and it was to the C. & C.C.S. that he turned in 1858 when the great increase of population during the gold rush made additional clergy essential.

Any action, we are told, calls forth an equal and opposite reaction and this rather one-sided interpretation of the Christian life was bound, sooner or later, to evoke a protest which would emphasise the Church as the Divine Society, the People of God, the Community of the Redeemed, whose ministry and sacraments were an important part of the way to salvation. The reaction came in what is variously described as the Oxford Movement or the Catholic Revival. The immediate occasion was the passing of the *Irish Church Bill* in 1833 which provided for the suppression of ten Irish bishoprics. Immediately afterwards the Reverend John Keble preached a sermon at Oxford which he entitled, "National Apostasy," and in which he spoke bitterly of "the fashionable liberality of this generation"[1] and pleaded that the Church was entitled to respect, not as a national institution, but as an instrument of the Divine Will. For laymen, such as the Prime Minister, to interfere with the pastoral authority of the bishops, the Successors of the Apostles, was a grievous sin; and a nation which fell into grievous sin could not expect protection of God. Ceremonial, or ritualism, was not at first a conspicuous part of the Catholic Revival but came later as a natural development. The teachings of those connected with the Oxford Movement were bitterly assailed in England not only because of their apparent novelty but also because they seemed to be playing into the hands of the Church of Rome and, needless to say, the fortunes of the movement were not helped by the secession of some of its leaders to the Roman obedience.

In British Columbia the conflict reached its climax in the unhappy controversy between the Bishop and the Dean in the early 1870's. Cridge, the Evangelical of unswerving conviction, had come as Hudson's Bay Company chaplain in 1855; Hills, supported by the S.P.G., and favourably disposed to the principles of the Catholic Revival, although by no means an extremist, had followed as Bishop in 1860. Thus, friction was not unlikely and it says something for both men that the situation did not become acute for a number of years. It has sometimes been suggested that part of Cridge's rancour was caused when he did not receive the episcopal appointment but there seems to be no documentary evidence to support this view.

In 1865 the Bishop selected Christ Church, Victoria, as his cathedral and Cridge was collated as Dean, an appointment which the Bishop admitted later was made, "only as an act of justice to the senior clergyman of the diocese, and minister of the church named to be the cathedral."[2]

The tension burst into open conflict on the occasion of the consecration of the new cathedral on Thursday, December 5th, 1872. At the evening service on that day the sermon was preached by the Venerable William Sheldon Reece, M.A., Archdeacon of Vancouver. The sermon seems to have been a moderate commendation of the new life which the Catholic Revival had brought to the Church, and a suggestion that reverence and devotion were deepened and increased by a degree of formality and ceremonial in the services in the Church. The Dean, however, took violent exception to what had been said and when he came forward to announce the hymn after the sermon, "remarked in a voice trembling with emotion that for seventeen years he had presided over Christ Church congregation and this was the first occasion on which Ritualism had been advocated. He raised his protest against the views advanced by Archdeacon Reece. They were wrong and he would not sit quietly and listen to their expression."[3]

Herein was the Dean's first grave mistake. Had he made his protest quietly and privately after the service all might have been well, but to contradict the sermon publicly was not only a lapse from Christian courtesy but a serious breach of canon law. The fact that the Bishop was present and with him the Bishop of Oregon and a number of visiting clergy made it impossible for the matter to be overlooked. A day or so later Dr. Hills wrote very gently to the Dean, remonstrating with him but leaving the way open for a gracious withdrawal.

Here the Dean made his second mistake by curtly refusing an apology and seeking to justify his behaviour. As a result the exchange of letters between Bishop and Dean continued. It might be wondered why the two men did not arrange to meet and to discuss the differences face to face but such a proceeding would have been alien to the etiquette of the day. The correct thing was to resolve the difficulty, if possible, by correspondence and consequently the Dean became more and more intransigent.

Meanwhile, numbers of letters relating to the incident appeared in the local press, but not one of them supported the Archdeacon's sermon while an editorial chided him for his indiscretion and bad taste in delivering the sermon "before a congregation notoriously hostile to the sentiments expressed by him."[4] It seems more than probable that some of the letters were instigated, if not written, by the Dean himself. All this gave the appearance of unanimous support of the Dean and, as another writer has pointed out,

> he was a Hudson's Bay Company chaplain before he was a Church rector. He had "the Company" solidly behind him. If he left the Church, many of the old stalwarts would leave with him. This is an interesting sidelight on the "family-company compact" influence in Victoria. Even in 1874 the Company's power was still felt. Cridge belonged to them; they would take care of him. Bishop Hills had no association with the company, he was regarded as an outsider.[5]

This seems to be an over-statement of the situation and it is probable that the Dean's associates supported him not because he was a "Company man" but because they agreed with his sentiments, never suspecting the lengths to which the dispute could take them.

The Dean persisted in his position and in order to sustain it

*Victoria District Church, later known as Christ Church, about 1858.*

*Bishop Cridge, 1885.*

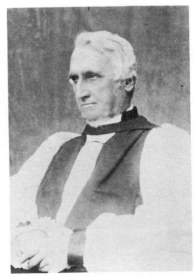

*Bishop Hills, about 1890.*

*The church at Metlakatla, dedicated in 1874.*

*Angela College, built in 1866.*

Right Reverend
Acton Windeyer
Sillitoe

Right Reverend W. Ridley

*The Iron Church (St. John's), Victoria, about 1910.*

*Church of St. John the Evangelist, Massett, Queen Charlotte Islands, consecrated May 7, 1887.*

fell back upon arguments which even he would have admitted, in more rational days, were contrary to Anglican belief and practice. The unhappy dispute dragged on for more than a year but finally came to a head when on January 9th, 1874, the Dean composed an open letter to the Bishop which was published in the Victoria papers on the following day. In it he affirmed first "that every local congregation, with its accepted pastor, is a complete church (the word and sacraments being duly ministered therein); that a Diocese is no necessary part of a Church,"[6] and, second, that the Bishop has no authority over a particular congregation. That the Cathedral congregation did not endorse the Dean's view is indicated by a resolution of the Church Committee passed a few days later: "That the Committee of Christ Church Cathedral having read the letter from the Very Rev. Dean Cridge to the Rt. Rev. the Bishop of Columbia published on the 10th of January, 1874, in the *Standard* and the *Colonist* on Synod, do not acquiesce in such a letter, and regret its publication."[7]

By this time the Dean seems to have reached a stage where reason had ceased to play any part in determining his policy. His sole concern had become to win the battle at all costs and to this end he rallied his forces at the annual vestry meeting in April, 1874, and secured the election of his own supporters to all the offices of the parish. Because of the Dean's continued opposition the Bishop, after a final warning, summoned him before an Ecclesiastical Court, in which the Bishop sat with four assessors, two clergymen and two County Court Judges. The Dean came and, although he protested the illegality of the court, took quite an active part in its proceedings frequently attempting to justify his position by reference to other ecclesiastical cases. Eighteen charges were brought against him and sixteen of them proved, leaving the Bishop no alternative but to suspend him. The suspension was published on September 22nd, 1874, but at the same time Cridge was given a final chance to acknowledge his errors.

The Bishop then announced to the churchwardens that he and his chaplain would conduct the services at the Cathedral on the following Sunday to which they curtly replied that arrangements had already been made for the rector to conduct them. Cridge himself wrote denying the authority of the Bishop to suspend him and intimating that competence to do so was vested in the law officers of the Crown. Victoria waited with baited breath to see what would happen on the following Sunday. The *Colonist,* which throughout the proceedings was strongly pro-Cridge, reported: "Yesterday notice was served on the Very Rev. Dean Cridge . . . informing the reverend gentleman that his license had been revoked. We believe we are correct in saying that no heed will be paid to the revocation, and that any attempt of the Lord Bishop to occupy the pulpit on Sunday next will be resisted by the Churchwardens and Committee. All things will be done decently and in order, but the attempt will be resisted."[8] The sincerity of the assurance that all things would be done decently and in order is by no means proved since the newspaper report of Sunday's proceedings seems to suggest a willingness to use force if necessary. The account reads, in part:

The announcement that Dean Cridge would disregard the illegal mandate of the Lord Bishop on Sunday morning attracted a large concourse of people to the sacred edifice which, some time before eleven o'clock, was full to overflowing. . . . The number of young, athletic looking men present was very large, and here and there on Church Hill were groups of Muscular Christians awaiting the progress of events. Just when the service was about to commence word came in that the Lord Bishop was preparing to leave for the Cathedral, and presently the pony carriage, containing the Bishop and Mrs. Hills, rolled out of Coutts Street; but instead of making for the Cathedral, the horse's head was turned Esquimalt-ward and it was announced that His Lordship had gone to officiate at St. Paul's. Everyone breathed freer; for no one wished a scene in or about the House of God—a "scene" that would have inevitably occurred had the Bishop carried out his expressed intention . . . of conducting the services at Christ Church morning and evening. It is well that he did not attempt to do so . . . .[9]

The Bishop had issued his order, and had been defied. There was therefore no alternative but for him to take the case to the Supreme Court and on October 18th he instituted proceedings. In the intervening days the *Colonist* continued to rail against what it described as episcopal persecution, and to defend the rebellious Dean. When the case came to court Mr. Chief Justice Begbie did his best to persuade the litigants to settle the matter out of court. In response to his suggestion, Cridge wrote a very inadequate letter of apology which was not acceptable to the Bishop since it covered only the initial incident and did not undertake full canonical obedience. On the following morning it was reported to the court that no satisfactory conclusion had been reached. On October 24th, the Chief Justice handed down his judgment in which he found for the Bishop, granting an injunction forbidding Cridge to exercise his ministry as rector of Christ Church, and as a clergyman of the Church of England.

Once again excitement ran high as the curious as well as the faithful waited to see what would happen on the following Sunday. When the time came Cridge and his family went to St. John's with many members of the Christ Church congregation. The Reverend F. B. Gribbell, Chaplain to the Bishop, arrived at the Cathedral to conduct the morning service, received the keys from the churchwarden and opened the doors. As he did so about seventy-five men and boys who had been standing near made their way into the cathedral and began carrying hymn-books, cushions, and hassocks from the pews on the instructions of the seat holders. As the service began there was no verger, no organist, two men in the choir, and a congregation of about twenty-five persons. Matins was read, a short sermon preached, and the congregation dismissed, but throughout the service parishioners were coming and going to take their possessions from the pews. The evening service proceeded in the same way, the same coming and going, an organist but no choir, and about 22 people in the congregation.

Cridge then announced that "not being able conscientiously to refrain from ministering he contemplated attaching himself to the Reformed Episcopal Church lately organized in Canada and the United States."[10] On October 29th, he and his supporters held a meeting which constituted the new church and services were begun in the Pandora Street Church on the following Sunday, November 1st. In this new undertaking he took with him "the Churchwardens, the whole of the Church Committee; the greater part of the congregation, and of the Sunday School, with the Superintendent and most of the Teachers; nearly all the choir with the organist; and the sexton. . . ."[11]

The *Columbia Mission Report*, 1874, made only a brief reference to the defection in the following terms: "We are sorry to say a clergyman who went out to British Columbia in 1855 as Chaplain to the Hudson [*sic*] Bay Company having been censured by the Bishop for disorderly conduct, and ultimately suspended, has seceded and joined a new sect lately commenced in the United States by a Dr. Cummins, drawing away at first a good many of his congregation. . . ."[12] The Report of the following year merely remarked that "the contributions of the cathedral in 1875 were but little below those of former days, notwithstanding the defections of Mr. Cridge and his adherents to the Cummins sect. . . ."[13]

Services of the new sect were continued in the Pandora Street

Church by Cridge and his followers until their new building, the Church of our Lord, was opened on January 16th, 1876. In 1875 Cridge took part in a ceremony which made him a bishop of the Reformed Episcopal body. The letters of consecration, handwritten on ordinary ruled foolscap, are preserved in the Provincial Archives, Victoria, together with the offer of the Presbyterian Theological College, Montreal, to confer upon him the degree of Doctor of Divinity (honoris cause) for his services in the Protestant cause. This degree was conferred on behalf of the College by the Rev. W. Leslie Clay in St. Andrew's Church, Victoria, on April 24th, 1895. Cridge himself gave the convo-cation address in which he reviewed the circumstances through which he and his followers had passed and acknowledged the giving of the degree as a tribute to his services for "the Church of the Protestant Reformation. . . ."[14]

Cridge himself died in 1913 but the schism which he created lived on and still survives. Although it is impossible to justify his inflexible obstinacy and difficult to sympathise with his refusal to admit himself even partly in the wrong, yet it must be remem-bered that Cridge was the child of his age. To him, the Oxford movement and all its works were but playing into the hands of the Church of Rome, and Rome was anathema, the source of all sorts of evil and mischief. Having refused to acknowledge his initial mistake until it was too late he was by circumstances backed into a corner and compelled to rely upon arguments which not even the most latitudinarian Anglican could tolerate. Here is one of the unresolved tensions of Anglicanism which must call forth the sympathetic understanding of all who acknowledge the claims of Christ.

---

1 J. R. H. Moorman, *A History of The Church in England*, A. & C. Black, London, 1952, p.338.
2 *Columbia Mission Report*, 1872.

3 *Daily British Colonist,* December 6th, 1872.
4 *Daily British Colonist,* December 8th, 1872.
5 Patricia M. Johnson, M.A., "McCreight and the Church," *B.C. Historical Quarterly,* Vol. XIII, No. 4, October, 1948, p.299.
6 *Daily British Colonist,* January 10th, 1874.
7 Minute Book of Christ Church Cathedral, January 16th, 1874, quoted by Patricia M. Johnson, op. cit.
8 *Daily British Colonist,* September 23rd, 1874.
9 *Daily British Colonist,* September 29th, 1874.
10 Minute Book of Christ Church Cathedral, October 27th, 1874, quoted by Patricia M. Johnson, op. cit., p.304.
11 Loc. cit.
12 *Columbia Mission Report,* 1874, p.18.
13 *Columbia Mission Report,* 1875, p.31.
14 *Daily British Colonist,* April 29th, 1895.

# 8

## The North Pacific Mission — A New Diocese

IN TRACING the story of missionary work in the north
Pacific we saw how William Duncan was sent out by the C.M.S.
to begin his work at Fort Simpson. Later he set up his model
village at Metlakatla where in his own peculiar way he cared for
the needs of the Indians, helping them to be self-reliant and able
to sustain themselves by crafts and commerce. We know, too,
that he ruled with a strict justice. Nor was the task an easy one,
for the Indians were a proud race and happy, for the most part,
with their own religion and traditions.

Perhaps the outstanding convert during this period was the
great Tsimshian chief, Legaic. He was the head chief of his
tribe and when Duncan first arrived had threatened his life, but
through the influence of the missionary's example and preaching
he had been converted and baptized with the Christian name,
Paul. After his baptism he had settled down and taken his place
as a carpenter in the village at Metlakatla. In his earlier days he

had been both ruthless and cruel and the story of one of his murders is worth telling as an indication of the sort of man he had been.

According to the story[1] there had been a long-standing feud between Legaic's family and another of the same tribe. Peace was made at the instance of Legaic who invited the members of the other family to come to a feast in his house in token of the re-establishment of amicable relations. The doors of the Indian houses are always very low, but Legaic nailed a piece of timber across the top of his door to make it lower still. Then he erected a wooden barrier inside the door so that those entering could not see inside. Having so done he dug a pit beyond the barrier and gave his sons their instructions.

At the time of the feast the guests, some six or eight men, arrived, approaching the door in single file. The leader entered with bowed head and one of the young men was ready to pull him suddenly forward. Down came the mighty club of Legaic on the back of his head, fracturing the skull. At the same instant one of the other young men dragged the body forward and threw it into the pit. The second was murdered in like manner, and the third, and all would have been similarly butchered had not one young man, following hard upon his predecessor, been startled to see him drop forward with a jerk. Drawing back, he was able to give warning to the others who escaped.

In 1873 there arrived at Metlakatla a young missionary from Ireland, William Henry Collison, who had just completed his training at the Church Missionary Training College at Islington. With him came his wife who was a deaconess, and who had served as a nurse in the Franco-Prussian war. For three years they helped with the work of the mission at Metlakatla and during this period Collison became deeply interested in the Haida Indians of the Queen Charlotte Islands. In the summer of 1876 he set out in a Haida-built canoe with a Tsimshian crew to visit them. The Haidas were unwilling to receive any missionaries, affirming their faith in the customs of their forefathers. The missionary felt, however, that the opposition had not been as strong as might have been expected, and thought that if he could teach the children he would be able to influence the parents through them.

With this in mind he returned to Metlakatla, packed up his belongings and with his wife and two children, made his way to Fort Simpson where he arranged with the Hudson's Bay Company steamer *Otter* to be taken to Massett. When the family reached their destination at the beginning of November, the captain of the ship put them ashore with the cheerful comment, "Well, I shall not be surprised to find you have all been murdered when I return again next year."[2]

But they were not murdered though progress was slow and difficult. As soon as they had settled themselves in a small log hut, they set out to learn the Haida language, and then to make provision for services and the opening of a school. All this time there was determined opposition from the medicine men, but when Collison was almost in despair, encouragement came suddenly and unexpectedly. A young chief named Cowhoe came to him carrying a book which he could not read but explaining that it had been given to him by the captain of the "fighting fire-ship."[3] The book proved to be a copy of the New Testament and on the fly-leaf was written:

> To the Indian Boy, Edenshaw's son,
> I trust that the bread cast upon
> the waters will soon be found.
>> James C. Prevost, Captain,
>> H.M.S. *Satellite*, 1859.[4]

Eighteen years had elapsed but the kindly words of a good man and his gift were used by God to be the turning point in the conversion of the Haida people to the light of the Christian Gospel.

In the autumn of 1877, as we have already seen, Bishop Bompas of Athabasca was asked by Bishop Hills to undertake the long and dangerous journey of nearly a thousand miles from Dunvegan on the Peace River to Metlakatla in order to ease the difficult situation which Duncan had created, and to confirm some of his converts. Bishop Bompas made the journey up and down rivers, along lakes and over portages, and finally down the Skeena, racing all the time against the approaching winter, so that when he reached the tidal waters at Port Essington he looked more like a battered miner than a bishop. At Metlakatla he confirmed 124 of the Christians and directed that communicants' classes be formed for them. On the way back he paused at Kincolith to admit Collison to the diaconte on March 17th, 1878. A week later he ordained him priest and placed him in charge of Metlakatla. The C.M.S. at once confirmed this appointment but after the Bishop had left, Duncan's authority was again exerted, and the Indians were refused the Holy Communion.

A year later, Bishop Hills was in England and, as we have seen, arrangements were completed for setting up the Diocese of Caledonia with the Right Reverend William Ridley as its first bishop. Bishop Ridley came to his diocese in the autumn of the same year expecting to receive a warm welcome, but finding instead that Duncan resented any questioning of his authority at Metlakatla even in matters ecclesiastical.

The Bishop was naturally concerned by the state of affairs and in order to avoid a premature rupture spent the winter of 1880-81 on the Skeena at Hazelton where he established a mission. None-the-less, such a condition could not continue and Duncan remained deaf to any ideas other than his own. In the words of the historian of the C.M.S.:

In church matters there was no improvement. Indeed Bishop Ridley found an unexpected absence of Christian instruction and privileges in the settlement. There were no Bible classes; there had been no attempt to give the people the Scriptures in their own tongue; while the children were taught English in the school, the adults were dependent on the Sunday addresses of Duncan and Collison—the latter having no power to institute new plans. The Sunday services—under police supervision—were practically the only religious ordinance; and the people were entirely absorbed in their fast-increasing worldly possessions.[5]

At length the C.M.S. felt it necessary to issue an ultimatum to their recalcitrant agent. Duncan was required either ( 1 ) to come to England at once for a conference, or ( 2 ) to facilitate the Bishop's plans for the religious instruction of the people, or ( 3 ) to hand over the Mission wholly to the Bishop, and leave the place. In reply, Duncan did none of these things, but instead he called the Indians together, assured himself of their support, and then openly defied the Bishop and the C.M.S. Not long afterwards, Duncan and his Indians came into conflict with the colonial authorities over questions of land tenure. In 1887, having quarreled with the authorities of both Church and State, Duncan and some five hundred of his followers took themselves off to establish a new Metlakatla in Alaska.

Much has been written about this unhappy situation and almost always Duncan has been represented as a hero, persecuted by a narrow-minded and bigoted church, although this is by no means the true picture. The Church was at fault to the extent that the C.M.S. was permitted a free hand without any episcopal supervision. The C.M.S. was at fault in appointing a new recruit to so grave a responsibility. But Duncan himself was greatly at fault in failing to remember that he occupied his post, not in any right of his own, but as a representative of his Church and Society. Regardless of what has been said, the North Pacific Mission was an Anglican venture, supported by Anglican funds, and those who laboured in it could justly be expected to teach the Faith as received by the Church of England. That Duncan could not—or would not—do so was reason enough for his removal.

Even during these troublesome times the work of the diocese was not at a standstill. Progress was being made in other areas and new mission stations established. The Reverend Charles Harrison was at Massett working on his translation of the Prayer Book into the Haida language; the Reverend R. W. Gurd at Kitkatla, and later at Metlakatla; and the Reverend John Field at Hazelton after a spell as a C.M.S. missionary in Ceylon.

The S.P.G. was represented by work at Port Essington, and Port Simpson on the coast, and at Atlin in the interior. To Port Essington, in 1884, came the Reverend A. H. Sheldon. Harold Sheldon had been a young doctor practising in Huddersfield when he heard the call to go to the desolate places. He was ordained and came to Caledonia where "for some years he led a wandering life, preaching the Gospel in the wilderness, rebuking sin unflinchingly, exercising his medical skill upon diseases: the diocese was his parish, and he travelled over it in canoes, or on foot, often weary, cold and hungry, seeking to reach men of whom no one else thought. Not a cent did he receive from anybody, or from any Society, until some commercial crash in the old land deprived him of his scanty funds."[6] Bishop Ridley found him in these conditions in 1884 and appointed him to Port Essington for which the S.P.G. had made a grant. There he worked with the same energy and enthusiasm, building a church at the Port, and still travelling far and wide. After three years of such work this "priest, doctor, traveller, sailor, the friend of all, died, as he would have chosen to die, in the work of his calling."[7] On the way to Fort Simpson, the new Indian canoe in which he was travelling was caught by a sudden gust of wind and split from stem to stern. The small vessel filled and then capsized. Sheldon and his crew of four Indians held on for a time, their hands caught in the split hull, but at last they fell off into the icy water. Only one lad, who got astride the hull, survived.

In 1889, two more missionaries were added to the list, the Reverend Alfred Edwin Price, whom the Bishop ordained and sent to Kitwanga, and the Reverend James Benjamin McCullagh, also ordained by Bishop Ridley, and sent to Aiyansh. Both men remained in their missions for long periods, caring for the Indians, learning their language, erecting the necessary mission buildings, and translating parts of the Bible and Prayer Book into the native tongue.

In the following year, the Reverend F. L. Stephenson, who had served in the diocese of British Columbia, volunteered for service in the Bulkley Valley and undertook to travel there on foot. This he did by following the route of the telegraph line, visiting all the cabins on the way. About the same time the Reverend John Henry Keen, who for seven years had served as C.M.S. missionary at Moose Fort, Hudson's Bay, was appointed to Massett and undertook the difficult task of compiling a grammar of the Haida language in which he was assisted by two natives, Mrs. Mary Ridley and Henry Edenshaw, son of the famous Chief Edenshaw.

In the early 90's Dr. Vernon Ardagh, who had served previously in East Africa, came to Metlakatla and after practising for a short time at Kisgyas on the Skeena river, returned to open a small hospital improvised from the two vacant native houses. About the same time a home was established, later to be known as the Ridley Home, for the children of isolated settlers and also for those of mixed blood.

There were, in the early days, few white residents but as the number of canneries increased, and the logging industry developed, the population increased, to be swollen still more by the gold rush of 1897 to the Klondyke. The S.P.G. voted a special sum to meet the emergency created by the gold rush, and Bishop Ridley took the Reverend Benjamin Appleyard and his wife from Port Essington, where they had been working, up to Glen-ora on the Stikine River where the miners loaded their pack animals for the long trail to the diggings. By the next year a rail-way had been completed from Skagway over the pass to Bennett City and the stream of travel changed to that route. There, within three days of the railway's opening were the Bishop and Apple-yard, and with them the Reverend F. L. Stephenson who was to minister to the miners at Atlin.[8]

In 1897 also, a new mission was opened at Tahl Tan, far up the Stikine river, by the Reverend F. M. T. Palgrave who stayed for four years[9] and then, it is said, made himself responsible for the stipend of his successor, the Reverend T. P. W. Thorman.

A disastrous fire occurred at Metlakatla on July 22nd, 1901, which destroyed the large church, the schools and homes, the Church Army Hall, the guesthouse for Indian visitors, the boat-houses with all the boats, and Bishop Ridley's own house with his library, manuscripts, records, Scripture translations, grammars and folk-lore. The men of the settlement were away at the time salmon fishing, and the women were alone to fight the fire. Bishop Ridley was in England at the time and when the news of the fire became known gifts poured in to help with the work of restora-tion. The Indians themselves also helped by contributing £350 in money, and labour to the value of £400. The new church was consecrated in October, 1903. When this had been done Bishop Ridley decided that it was time for him to retire, and he returned to England alone, his wife having died in Metlakatla in 1896.

In all such work the wife is as much a missionary as her husband, and Mrs. Ridley who had been a true helpmate to the Bishop in this respect, was beloved by all the native women. She had suffered intense pain during her last few months but was always sympathetic and interested when her native friends called to see her, and enquired about their general welfare. When she died they asked that she be buried in their own churchyard.

The first chapter in the history of the Diocese of Caledonia was over. It had been a period of evangelization of the native peoples, but a new era was soon to begin with the building of the Grand Trunk Pacific Railway and the opening up of the interior to white settlers. The C.M.S. decided to look to Canada for the next bishop, partly with the thought that this distant diocese should be brought more fully into the life of the Canadian Church. Their choice fell upon the Reverend Frederick Herbert Du Vernet, a native of Quebec, who had served in the diocese of Montreal and Toronto, and had been a member of the faculty of Wycliffe College, Toronto. In addition, he had been keenly interested in the C.M.S., secretary-treasurer of its Canadian Auxiliary and editor of the *Canadian Church Missionary Gleaner*. He was consecrated in Christ Church Cathedral, Montreal, on St. Andrew's Day, 1904.

His reception, on arrival in his new diocese, was very different from that which had been accorded to Bishop Ridley as missionaries and populace alike were very glad to see him. Bishop Du Vernet lost no time in visiting his new field of labour, going first to see Archdeacon Collison, and then over the ice to Aiyansh on the Upper Nass River to seeMcCullagh. Few white men had ever attempted this journey in winter but the Bishop felt amply repaid when, although surprised by his arrival, the missionary had candidates ready for confirmation. This was the first confirmation service to be held at Aiyansh. Going down the river on the return journey, the Bishop visited Lakalzap, now Greenville, and was impressed by the way the Indian people conducted the services. He was also greatly touched as they explained that they had called their newly-built church St. Andrew's because that was the day of his consecration. By August, 1905, the Bishop had visited all but the most remote missions in his diocese and, at that time, left for the sessions of the General Synod at Quebec. This was the first time that the Diocese of Caledonia had been so represented.

The next important event in the life of the diocese was the first meeting of the diocesan synod at Metlakatla on August 21st, 1906. A number of conferences had been held previously but now, for the first time, the synod was duly established.

About this time it became known that a second transcontinental railway was planned, and that its western terminus would be in Caledonia. This would mean, as one writer pointed out, that "the Indians would profit materially, but it will not foster their spiritual life. The simplicity of the early converts must inevitably be lost; and we must not be surprised if the reports on the congregations continue to be, as they have been lately, less favourable than formerly."[10] When the site of the new terminus was chosen at a place six miles from Metlakatla, Bishop Du Vernet was ready to meet the needs of incoming settlers. Prince Rupert sprang into being and with it, St. Andrew's Church Hall, the forerunner of the present cathedral. This was in 1907, and in the same year the Bishop transferred his headquarters from Metlakatla to Prince Rupert.

The whole country was optimistic, and so was the Bishop,[11] Prince Rupert had grown to be a good sized town, with Smithers, Telkwa and Houston developing similarly. Then came the war of 1914-1918 with its challenge and its difficulties. Pews became empty, clergy left to serve as chaplains to the forces and promising parishes were vacant.

After the completion of the railway, the Bishop was able to visit the area in the far eastern part of his diocese known as the Peace River Block. He went by train as far as Edson, Alberta, and then directly north over the old Edson trail. He covered the distance partly on foot and partly by wagon, visiting the settlers along the way, and seeing the country for himself. Two years later he made the journey again but this time going by way of Edmonton and the new railway to Pouce Coupe which had just been completed. There he visited the Reverend John Henry Kerr who, after a brief spell in the diocese of Toronto, had just begun his work as priest-in-charge of the Peace River District. Land had been secured for a church at Kilkerran and there, it is said, the Bishop knelt with a handful of settlers and prayed that the Cross of Christ would one day be established in "the Block."

Soon after the war the soldier settlements were established in various districts as, for example, at Chilco near Vanderhoof, and at Burns Lake, but the spirit of optimism which had prevailed before the war was now lacking, and life had become a grim struggle for existence. It was at this point that Archbishop Du Vernet died. At the establishment of the Ecclesiastical Province of British Columbia in 1915 he had been elected Metropolitan and Archbishop. Of his part in the establishment of the ecclesiastical province, and of his contribution to the Anglican Theological College we shall speak later. Suffice it to say here that in the diocese of Caledonia his episcopate was one of expansion and building. New areas were opening up, new churches were being built. The coming of the railway and the first Great War changed the whole face of the diocese and necessitated new ways of working.

1 Told by the Reverend John Sheepshanks, in D. W. Duthie, *A Bishop in the Rough*, Smith, Elder & Co., London, 1909, p.151.
2 W. H. Collison, *In the Wake of the War Canoe*, E. P. Dutton & Co., New York, 1916, p.121.

3 *Ibid.*, p.173.
4 loc. cit.
5 Eugene Stock, *History of the Church Missionary Society*, C.M.S., London, 1899, Vol. III, p.251.
6 H. P. Thompson, *Into All Lands*, S.P.C.K., London, 1951, p.267.
7 *Ibid.*, p.268.
8 *Ibid.*, p.269.
9 Alice J. Janvrin [Ed.] *Snapshots of the North Pacific*, C.M.S., London, 1904, p.140.
10 E. Stock, op. cit., IV, 388.
11 For much of the general information towards the end of this chapter I am indebted to a pamphlet entitled: *Diocese of Caledonia: 1879-1950*.

# 9

# New Westminster

# And the Interior

ACTON Windeyer Sillitoe, M.A. (Cantab.), was consecrated the first Bishop of New Westminster in Croydon Parish Church on All Saints' Day, 1879.

He spent some months in England after his consecration, organizing a home committee, addressing missionary meetings in various parts of the country, and generally trying to interest people in the work of the new diocese. At the end of April, 1880, he and Mrs. Sillitoe left England. They crossed the continent by Union Pacific to San Francisco, the only trans-continental railway line in those days. The couple were then carried from San Francisco to Victoria by the steamer *Idaho*, crowded to capacity with men going to work on the construction of the Canadian Pacific Railway. After a few days rest with Bishop and Mrs. Hills in Victoria, the last leg of the journey to New Westminster was accomplished.

They arrived in their new see city on June 18th, and were met by the Venerable C. T. Woods, Archdeacon of Columbia, and rector of Holy Trinity, New Westminster, and the Reverend Charles R. Baskett, who was described as "Missionary at Hastings."[1] In addition to these two, the Reverend George Ditcham, priest-in-charge at Hope and Chilliwack, and the Reverend J. B. Good, S.P.G. Missionary at Yale and Lytton, completed the diocesan clergy staff. After conferring with the clergy the Bishop began to visit some of the settlements and logging camps where there was no priest. Obviously there were many of these. Almost invariably he was accompanied on the longer trips by Mrs. Sillitoe who seems to have kept a full account of their travels. Unfortunately, the Sillitoe papers have disappeared but a significant part of their descriptions of travelling conditions and life in the province has been preserved in H. H. Gowen's *Church Life in British Columbia,* and in two small pamphlets published by Mrs. Sillitoe after the Bishop's death.[2]

From these sources we learn that one of the Sillitoes' first trips was into the interior and took them into the southern Okanagan. Having made their way to Hope by river steamer, they made arrangements with two Indians, Antoine and Susap, to supply them with guides and horses for twenty-four dollars a day, and to guide them over the trails to Osoyoos. The trails were rough and hazardous and sometimes there were streams to ford or fallen trees to climb over. Each evening, in the absence of any established stopping places, they made beds of fir and cedar and in the cold and frosty mountain air lay down for the night. Under such conditions they travelled for a week or ten days until at last they came to Osoyoos. There, on Sunday, September 19th, 1880, the Bishop held a service to which all the settlers came. Even when they were all present, however, there were not more than a dozen or so!

Between Osoyoos and Penticton the Bishop and his party had an adventure which, reported Mrs. Sillitoe, came near to ending our earthly career. We were asleep in our tent when we were awakened by a hurried call from the Indian. There was a curious, rumbling noise which grew louder and louder, very much like an earthquake, and the ground seemed to shake beneath one's feet. The night was dark and, standing in the door of one's tent, it was impossible at first to see anything, but a cloud passing away from the face of the moon revealed a band of wild horses bearing down upon us at full gallop. As they came near and saw us they divided into two groups, passing by on either side. Had the moon not come out they would have probably become entangled in our tent ropes and we should not have lived to tell the tale.[3]

At last they reached Penticton and met Thomas Ellis and his family who had been in the district since 1865. Each Sunday afternoon it had been their custom to gather in the drawing room with their friends and neighbours for a religious service which would be taken by Ellis himself, or a member of the family, except on the rare occasions when a clergyman or minister was present. After the services at Penticton the Bishop and Mrs. Sillitoe went their way on horseback to Sunnyside, now known as Westbank, where they stayed with the Allisons and baptized some of their children. Thence they made their way to Vernon and eventually to Kamloops. At each place the ordinary services were held, often there were baptisms, and nearly always there were enquiries about the appointment of a resident priest—a plea which the Bishop was all too often reluctantly compelled to refuse because of the scarcity of clergy and of funds to maintain them. From Kamloops the Bishop returned by way of Ashcroft, which Gowen described as "a very English settlement, for two of the farmers were found keeping a pack of foxhounds with which to hunt the coyotes"![4] Towards the end of October it was reported in the *Inland Sentinel* that "Bishop Sillitoe has returned to Yale after visiting the interior country; and delivered a discourse on Sunday evening, . . . to a large audience, in the interest of the fund for the recent addition to St. John's Church. Both the Bishop and his lady speak highly of the country and the people they travelled through."[5] The incumbent at Yale at the time was the Reverend John Booth Good who had just enlarged the church by the addition of the chancel. When he moved to Lytton, Good's place was taken by the Reverend Darrel W. H. Horlock, a young Englishman who after a stay of two years was moved by the Bishop to Kamloops—an indication of the growth of population in the interior. It is interesting to note, by comparison, that the newspaper, the *Inland Sentinel*, followed a similar course of movement, beginning at Emory's Bar in 1880, moving to Yale later in the year, and then finding its permanent home in Kamloops in 1884.

Kamloops had been established as a fur-trading post in 1812, and for several years after 1884 it was the centre of Anglican missions in the area. Horlock, who stayed there until 1887, was joined by the Reverend Alfred Shildrick and the Reverend Henry Irwin who, generally known by his nickname, Father Pat, has become a legend throughout the interior. Between them they maintained services in what was vaguely known as the Kamloops Missionary District which included everything south of Kamloops to the international boundary and east to the summit of the Rocky Mountains as well as Ashcroft and the Nicola valley. Horlock's comment on his return from one missionary journey was both an indication of the distances to be travelled and an interesting comment on the prevailing conditions. "Rev. Mr. Horlock," ran the report, "has returned from Eagle Pass and as far as Farwell [Revelstoke]. He reports a bad state of affairs; the liquor traffic is extensive, and scenes that are disgraceful to civilization are too frequently witnessed. The Government is not doing its duty and serious consequences may follow."[6] In the following year there was a reference to a journey to the southern

Okanagan. "The Rev. D. Horlock returned on Thursday last from a mission trip to Keremeos and Penticton. At the former place he was the guest of Mr. and Mrs. Cawston whose first-born son he baptized. He also consecrated the grave of the late Mr. Lowe, whose body has lately been removed to a beautiful spot on Mr. Cawston's estate."[7]

A store was converted to serve as a temporary church in Kamloops, and when Horlock returned to England in 1887 he was succeeded by the Reverend Canon W. H. Cooper, F.R.G.S., who had served the church in Australia, and more recently in Manitoba and Saskatchewan. He had been made a canon of the Diocese of Saskatchewan by Bishop McLean. Immediately after his arrival, Canon Cooper set out on horseback for a three-week trip which took him through the southern Okanagan to Penticton, then west to Keremeos and Princeton, and back to Kamloops by way of the Nicola valley. On his return he reported that the trip had been very successful, the country through which he had passed seemed well-settled and prosperous, and that he had "completed arrangements to have services held once every two months at the outlying stations near the American border, and at those near Kamloops once a month."[8]

Some two years previously, in April, 1885, the Reverend Alfred Shildrick had married Miss Alice Henrietta Innes, of Esquimalt and they had moved to a new parsonage at Spallumcheen (Enderby). Shildrick, still an assistant priest of the Kamloops Missionary District, was then responsible for "Spallumcheen, Priest's Valley, and the Mission, with occasional visits to Penticton and Osoyoos."[9] In 1890 when Canon Cooper returned to England, Shildrick was appointed to Kamloops, and the Okanagan Missionary District was set up with the Reverend T. Williams Outerbridge, formerly of Banff and Mitford, as priest-in-charge. Almost at once the district was divided and a second priest in the person of the Reverend Thomas Greene, B.A., who had been serving in the Diocese of Qu'Appelle, was appointed to minister to the southern Okanagan.

It was natural that any priest coming to that area should find his way first to Penticton where the Ellis family had been settled for nearly thirty years and where, in 1892, they had caused a church to be built. In 1891 the members of the family had been involved in a serious accident when their horses became fright-ened on the way to Kamloops. In thanksgiving for their escape from death Ellis had the church built on his property and sug-gested for it the appropriate name, St. Saviour.

The first service in the building was held on April 26th, 1892, and on November 6th its sanctuary was dedicated by Bishop Sillitoe, and early in the following year Greene assumed charge of the parish. Soon after his arrival in Penticton, Greene heard that there was a settlement of English people in and about Kelowna and in May, 1894, began to hold monthly services there with the result that St. Michael's church was built and opened in October, 1895.

Meanwhile, Outerbridge had taken up residence in Vernon (formerly known as Priest's Valley) which took its name from a pioneer church family, that of G. Forbes Vernon. The first church in Vernon, dedicated to All Saints', was built by Edwin Harris, and used for the first time on April 30th, 1893. Shortly after the opening of the church, Outerbridge moved to St. Paul's, Vancouver, but returned in the following year and remained as rector of Vernon until 1900, when he was succeeded by the Reverend J. H. Lambert, M.A.

In this way the Church in the Okanagan continued to grow. New parishes and missions were established, churches built, and clergy appointed, until the time came for the establishment of the Diocese of Kootenay. Meanwhile, the Church was continuing to grow in other parts of the diocese, and by 1889, ten years after its formation, the list of parishes was as follows:

| Parish | Communicants | Clergy |
|---|---|---|
| Holy Trinity, | 180 | The Bishop |
| New Westminster | | Rev. H. Irwin |
| St. James, Vancouver | 222 | Rev. H. G. Fiennes-Clinton |
| with Moodyville | | Rev. H. Edwardes |
| Christ Church, Vancouver | 160 | Rev. H. P. Hobson |
| All Saints', Trenant | 18 | Rev. C. Croucher |
| Christ Church, Surrey | 90 | Rev. W. Bell |
| St. Mary's, Sapperton | (no return) | Ven. C. T. Woods |
| Fraser River Missionary District | 34 | Rev. G. Ditcham |
| St. Thomas', Chilliwack | 32 | Rev. W. B. Allen |
| St. John, Yale (white) | 17 | The Bishop |
| Yale, (Indian) | 28 | Rev. R. Small |
| | | Rev. E. L. Wright |
| Lytton District (white) | 12 | The Bishop |
| St. Paul's, Lytton (Indian) | 400 | Rev. R. Small |
| | | Rev. E. L. Wright |
| Kamloops Missionary District | 100 | Rev. F. E. Wright |
| St. Saviour's, Cariboo | 17 | Rev. F. D. Brookes [10] |

With the completion of the Canadian Pacific Railway to Port Moody in 1885 the population of the lower mainland had increased rapidly, and with the opening of a branch line to Vancouver two years later the development was even greater. One of the most significant aspects was the emergence of the city of Vancouver. Prior to the coming of the railway there had been two settlements on the shores of Burrard Inlet—Granville and Hastings, not to mention Moodyville on the north shore—and in these the Church had carried on her ministrations. In Granville, St. James' Church had been built and dedicated on May 15th, 1881, only to be destroyed by fire in 1886. Under the leadership of the Reverend H. G. Fiennes-Clinton, who was rector from 1885 until his death in 1912, the church was rebuilt and consecrated on New Year's Day, 1888. In passing, it is amusing to note that Clinton was not impressed by the pretensions of the new town of Vancouver. In a letter of 1886 he wrote to a friend,

> Lately we have changed our name from the pleasing one of Granville to the bombastic, swaggering title of Vancouver. It is called this because it is the terminus of the Canadian Pacific Railway, and the C.P.R. are so fond of high-sounding names, that Granville did not suit them so they changed it to another which will create much confusion as there is, [*sic*] besides Vancouver Island, two other places in the States, one quite near, also called Vancouver. However all the swagger in the world will not build houses, and if they don't mend soon they will have this place a city of shanties, without water, roads, or drains. Drains there are none whatever that does not matter as no one ever gets ill here so the four poor idle doctors say. The roads are quite impassable from the mudholes till this week when a bit of glorious weather has improved matters, though still leaving some awful mudholes, so bad that even a shortlegged man on horseback can hardly keep his feet out of the mud . . . .[11]

St. James' Church, to return to it, had been established with a moderately high church tradition, which became the tradition of a large part of the diocese of New Westminster with the support and blessing of Bishop Sillitoe himself. Father Clinton, however, was sage enough to see that as Vancouver grew there would be people of other schools of thought to whom such a tradition might not appeal. In consequence, when the time came to establish a second parish he deliberately suggested that it might be somewhat less ornate in its worship and ceremonial. As a result, Christ Church, Vancouver, came into being in 1888 with the Reverend H. P. Hobson, a recent graduate of Wycliffe College, Toronto, as the first rector.

The city was developing so rapidly that in the following year two mission churches were built at some distance from Christ

W. DICKES.

CHURCH AND CLERGYMAN'S LOG HUT AT NEW WESTMINSTER.

*An engraving from The Columbia Mission Report, 1861*

Church—St. Michael's on Mount Pleasant, and St. Paul's on Hornby Street. Before long both these were self-supporting and other parishes were being established.

It was at this point, on June 9th, 1894, that Bishop Sillitoe died of pneumonia brought on by anxiety and overwork. Not only had he carried out long and arduous visitations of the diocese as bishop but he had been constantly harrassed by financial anxieties which made it necessary for him to serve as well as rector of Holy Trinity, New Westminster, and in February, 1892, he had undertaken a deputation tour in eastern Canada in very trying circumstances. He was deeply loved by all whose lives he touched.

The Bishop's influence for good extended beyond purely ecclesiastical concerns and he was one of the moving spirits in the establishment of the provincial university. In the spring of 1890, he wrote, "A Bill is before the local House for the incorporation of a British Columbia University. It seems doubtful, however, if a Bill will be proceeded with this year. The subject is a most important one, and cannot adequately be dealt with in the hurry of an expiring session. . . . One particular point does not appear to have been raised, *viz.* the locality of the University. There will probably be a good deal of discussion upon this point."[12]

The Bill passed, however, and the first meeting of Convocation was held in Victoria in August of the same year with Bishop Sillitoe in the chair. At that time it was decided to hold a further meeting in Vancouver to consider necessary amendments to the new University Act. This second meeting was held on October 22nd, in the Court House, with Bishop Sillitoe again acting as chairman. After calling on the Secretary to read some official announcements of appointments recently made under the new Act, the Bishop requested the newly-appointed Chancellor, Dr.

Israel W. Powell, to take the chair. A vote of thanks was passed to the Bishop "for so ably and kindly having acted as chairman of their first convocation."[13]

In the interests of the Church as a whole Bishop Sillitoe was active in the formation of the General Synod. A preliminary meeting which has come to be known as the Winnipeg Conference was held in that city on August 15th, 1890 at the suggestion of the Provincial Synod of Canada. Among those present were the Reverend E. S. W. Pentreath, of Winnipeg, later to become Archdeacon of Columbia; the Venerable C. T. Woods, Archdeacon of Columbia; and Lacey Johnson, a layman of New Westminster.[14] Two resolutions were passed by this conference, first, "that this Conference is of the opinion that it is expedient to unite and consolidate the various branches of the Church of England in British North America," and second, "that in any scheme of union the Conference affirms the necessity of the retention of provinces under a General Synod."[15] Interestingly enough, Bishop Hills of British Columbia, although he supported the idea of a general synod at first,[16] later became strongly opposed to any such scheme and said so repeatedly, while Bishop Sillitoe welcomed it and worked for it as a mark of development in the Canadian Church. There seems to be no extant comment from Bishop Ridley of Caledonia, but as he took no part in the proceedings of General Synod it is to be supposed that he was not interested.

The first session of the General Synod held its opening service in St. Alban's Cathedral, Toronto, on September 13th, 1893, and then assembled for business sessions in Trinity College, at which Biship Sillitoe was active in resolving differences and promoting the well-being of the new synod. The Archbishop of Rupert's Land, in addressing his own synod afterwards, spoke gratefully of the assistance Bishop Sillitoe had rendered in these initial meetings, while the Canadian *Church Guardian* commented: "We feel sure that every one who took part in that historic meeting will be glad to find this now open tribute paid to the late Lord Bishop of New Westminster, whose strong personality and wise judgment, as well as winning manner, impressed itself upon all who were present [at the first General Synod], and won so great a benefit for the Church in Canada."[17] As a mark of appreciation Bishop Sillitoe was invited to preach the sermon at the closing service on thanksgiving on Monday, September 18th. He was also awarded the degree of D.C.L. (*honoris causa*) by Trinity College.

At his death a few months later many tributes were offered, not the least significant of which came from the Bishop of Nova Scotia:

> A man of solid learning and many gifts, he never spared himself in any way if he might do or say something which would further the work committed to his trust, the establishing and extending of the Church in the newly-created diocese, including all the southern half of the mainland of British Columbia, and containing an area of 186,000 square miles, . . . Is it any wonder that fourteen years and a half of such work, in such a field, should have sufficed to cut short, before its time, a life full of great blessing, and to arrest a career which contained the elements of greatness.[18]

At the synod held to elect a successor, the Reverend W. Hibbert Binney, Vicar of Witton, Cheshire, and a son of the late Bishop of Nova Scotia, was nominated but felt unable to accept the invitation extended to him. The Bishops of Columbia and Caledonia were then asked to make the appointment in consultation with the Bishops of London, Norwich, and St. Alban's. Their choice fell upon the Reverend John Dart, M.A. (Oxon.), D.C.L., who had been President of King's College, Windsor, N.S., and who was at the time organizing secretary of the S.P.G. in the diocese of Manchester. He was consecrated in St. Paul's

Cathedral, London, on St. Peter's Day, 1895, and arrived in New Westminster with his wife and four sons in the following August. The situation in the diocese when he arrived was critical. The episcopal income was almost non-existent, and the nineteen clergy were dispirited and divided, but the Bishop worked with constant effort and unflinching courage. In addressing the Synod the Bishop said,

> Before I accepted the Bishopric, on the invitation of the Archbishop of Canterbury, I had sent to me what seemed to be an official statement, which showed me that I might count upon an income sufficient, with rigid economy, to live upon. But the income has never approached the point indicated. I found myself in possession of a large and expensive house, heavily mortgaged, with an income insufficient to begin with and rapidly diminishing, and with no fund to draw upon for the travelling and other expenses incidental to my office.[19]

The difficulty occurred largely because the endowment fund was invested in real estate in New Westminster and this, in consequence of the general depression, had virtually ceased to yield any income.[20]

In the circumstances it was natural enough that he should turn for aid to the S.P.G. under whose auspices the Bishopric Endowment Fund had been set up. In addition, he formed a New Westminster Missionary Association in England which, with the support and guidance of his commissaries, was of great help. His commissaries at the time were the Reverend Canon R. Rhodes Bristow, M.A., who arranged for meetings and other public functions in London, and the Reverend Jerome Mercier, Rector of Kemerton, who worked away quietly in the country near Tewkesbury. When Mercier died in 1901, the Bishop invited the Reverend H. G. Cundy, D.D., to become Commissary in his stead. Mrs. Jerome Mercier continued to work indefatigably for the English Association and with her son, the Reverend J. A. B.

Mercier, visited British Columbia a few years later. When the diocese of Kootenay came into being the title was changed to include both dioceses, and it became the New Westminster and Kootenay Missionary Association.

Quite early in the present century it was felt that the work in England had grown to the extent that an organizing secretary was needed. On the recommendation of his commissaries the Bishop appointed the Reverend Jocelyn H. T. Perkins, M.A., Minor Canon of Westminster Abbey who immediately threw himself with much enthusiasm into the work. It was his hope to appoint a local secretary in each archdeaconry in England, and to build up a body of speakers and workers who would enlist others in support of the Dioceses of New Westminster and Kootenay.

In 1905 the committee of the English Association deemed it wise to amalgamate with the S.P.G. which was still making substantial contributions to the work in British Columbia. Such amalgamation was being undertaken by similar societies both to avoid any possible friction and to consolidate the efforts being made. As a result all moneys collected by the Association, except those for the Bishopric Endowment Funds, were to be paid over to the treasurers of the S.P.G. who would distribute them in accordance with the wishes of the donors and the Association. Moreover, all missionaries who had been supported by the Association would now become agents of the S.P.G. with the attendant privileges and responsibilities.[21]

With the approach of the Jubilee of Bishop Hills' consecration the English Association felt that some worthy commemoration should be arranged and decided that in addition to services and meetings there should be a Jubilee Thankoffering, the proceeds of which would be devoted to the proposed St. Mark's Theological College, Vancouver.[22] Further reflection led them

*Holy Trinity Church, New Westminster, about 1860.*

*Chinese gold mining with a rocker at Boston Bar about 1860.*
*This is from a drawing by the Reverend W. B. Crickmer.*

to see that the matter was too large to be undertaken solely by themselves, and the co-operation of the Columbia Missionary Association was sought. A joint committee was set up which had among its members the Honourable H. J. Turner, Agent General for British Columbia; Miss Perrin, sister of the Bishop of British Columbia; the Reverend W. H. P. Arden, a nephew of Bishop Hills; and the Reverend Jocelyn Perkins.

The celebrations were arranged to coincide as nearly as possible with the actual date of Bishop Hills' consecration fifty years earlier. The service, consisting of a "Procession and High Celebration,"[23] was held at St. Peter's, Eaton Square, on February 23rd, since the following day, the actual anniversary of the consecration, was Ash Wednesday. At the service were the Bishop of Moosonee, Bishop Ridley who had retired from the see of Caledonia, Bishop Montgomery, the Secretary of the S.P.G., and many clergy who had worked in British Columbia or were interested in the work there. The sermon by the Bishop of Stepney on Psalm 112, verses 4-9, was a commemoration of the life and labours of Bishop Hills. The meeting on the following day was held at the Mansion House with the Lord Mayor of London in the chair, calling to mind those meetings which Bishop Hills himself had organized in support of the Columbia Mission before leaving for his new diocese. The Bishop of Norwich (Sheepshanks) sent his greetings, saying, "I believe I am the only one still living of the band of men who fifty years ago went forth from the Mansion House."[24]

At the conclusion of the Jubilee Year another great service of Thanksgiving was held, this time in St. Paul's Cathedral, on January 31st, 1910, with the Bishop of London, the Right Reverend A. F. Winington-Ingram, always a keen supporter, as the preacher. This service, too, was followed by a meeting at the Mansion House at which a resolution was passed asking that "the organization formed to carry out the Jubilee Commemoration of the Church in British Columbia be made permanent, the Societies already existing at home on behalf of the various dioceses being invited to unite with it preserving, if desired, their separate individuality."[25] Negotiations between the various committees followed and by the end of 1910 the British Columbia Church Aid Society was formed with a central committee, and committees for each of the four dioceses. The Reverend Jocelyn Perkins remained as General Secretary. In 1913 the Society's sphere of action was extended to include the Diocese of Yukon, and the appropriate change made in its title. Through the years the British Columbia and Yukon Church Aid Society has laboured continuously for the work of the Church in the Province, for the episcopal endowment funds, and for the Provincial Theological College.

Bishop Dart died in 1910 and was succeeded by the Right Reverend A. U. de Pencier, M.A., who had become Rector of St. Paul's, Vancouver, in 1908. Two of the most notable incidents in the early years of his episcopate were the removal of the Cathedral to Vancouver, and the establishment of the Kennington Mission to the Cariboo.

First, matters connected with the See House and Cathedral. Bishop Sillitoe had constituted Holy Trinity Church, New Westminster as the Cathedral of the diocese in October, 1892, but the action was rescinded by his successor, the Right Reverend John Dart, in May, 1898. Almost immediately after Bishop de Pencier's consecration he realised that the See House and Cathedral were no longer in the heart of the diocese. "After a year's residence in the City of New Westminster," he wrote, "in the See House which had been occupied by both my predecessors in the days when Vancouver was a small town, I came to the conclusion that it was essential for the proper discharge of my work to live nearer the centre of population, which is now the City of Vancouver."²⁶ With this in mind a house was secured for the temporary occupancy of the Bishop and property bought near where St. John's, Shaughnessy, now stands for development as a cathedral foundation. Not unnaturally the people of New Westminster were bitterly disappointed and, unfortunately, challenged the ownership of the See House and the Bishop's right to make any change. Ultimately the matter was resolved but no new cathedral was built. Instead, in 1929, Christ Church, Vancouver, was designated as the cathedral and a special canon passed by the diocesan synod allowing Holy Trinity, New Westminster, to be "by courtesy designated Holy Trinity Cathedral in perpetuity, although not being the Cathedral of the Diocese."²⁷

The Kennington Mission found its inspiration in the vision of the Reverend Canon Edward Brooke, M.A., Rector of St. John the Divine, Kennington, London, who encouraged his two curates, the Reverend C. T. Pelham and the Reverend W. B. Drake; the Reverend R. H. Isaac Williams, assistant curate of St. Stephen's, Kensington; and two laymen, Messrs. S. Pollinger and W. Goodman; to undertake work in Cariboo, at the same time promising financial and spiritual support for five years. The party arrived at Quesnel on the eve of Whitsunday, 1911, having driven some 230 miles up the Cariboo Road from Ashcroft.

When they arrived it was to discover that the only available building was a Union Church used by the Presbyterians. The Eucharist was celebrated there on Whitsunday after which the services were held in a barn until, soon afterwards, it was possible to buy the Union Church and move it to the mission property until a permanent church could be built. The mission house itself was built as a memorial to Canon Brooke who died soon after the undertaking began and was completed by Christmas, 1912. From Quesnel, the mission spread to Fort George on the Fraser

River where a small church dedicated to St. George was built. Another church, St. Stephen's, was subsequently built in South Fort George about three miles from its neighbour. Services were also held at St. Saviour's, Barkerville after a lapse of some years, and at 150 Mile House. In addition, one of the Mission priests made more or less regular journeys through the Chilcotin country. During 1913, the new church of St. John the Divine, Quesnel, was dedicated by the Archdeacon of Yale, the Venerable E. W. W. Pugh.

In 1914, at the outbreak of war, Bishop de Pencier felt obliged to offer his services as a Chaplain to the Forces and for the next three years the diocese was administered by the Venerable F. C. C. Heathcote, who had succeeded Archdeacon Pentreath, with the assistance of neighbouring bishops.

1 *Columbia Mission Report*, 1879, Clergy list.
2 H. H. Gowen, *Church Work in British Columbia*, Longmans, Green, London, 1899. *Early Days in British Columbia*, 1922, and *Pioneer Days in British Columbia*, no date, by Violet E. Sillitoe.
3 *Early Days in British Columbia*, p.12.
4 Gowen, op. cit., p.25.
5 *Inland Sentinel*, October 28th, 1880.
6 *Inland Sentinel*, September 10th, 1885.
7 *Inland Sentinel*, November 7th, 1886.
8 *Inland Sentinel*, October 15th, 1887.
9 Letter from the Reverend Alfred Shildrick, *Churchman's Gazette*, January, 1886, p.248.
10 *Churchman's Gazette*, Vol. IX, No. 11, pp.684-5.
11 From an original letter in the City Archives, Vancouver, by the courtesy of the Archivist, Major J. S. Matthews.
12 *Churchman's Gazette*, Vol. X, No. 1, April, 1890, p.703.
13 *Churchman's Gazette*, Vol. X, No. 8, November, 1890, p.757.
14 Robert Machray, *Life of Robert Machray*, Macmillan, Toronto, 1909, photograph between pages 368-9.
15 C. W. Vernon, *The Old Church in the New Dominion*, S.P.C.K., London, 1929, p.181.
16 Proceedings of The Synod of the Diocese of British Columbia, 1888, p.14.

17 Gowen, op. cit., p.207.
18 *Ibid.*, p.227.
19 *Work for the Far West*, January, 1898, p.4.
20 *Ibid.*, p.19.
21 *Work for the Far West*, July, 1905, pp.18 & 23.
22 *Work for the Far West*, July, 1908, p.13.
23 *Work for the Far West*, April, 1909, p.14.
24 British Columbia Church Aid Society, *Year Book*, 1911, p.63.
25 *Ibid.*, p.19.
26 British Columbia Church Aid Society, *Year Book*, 1913, p.115
27 Proceedings, Synod of the Diocese of New Westminster, June, 1914, p.32.

# 10

# Adventure in
# Kootenay

THE Reverend Henry Irwin, more commonly known as Father Pat, is a legend in British Columbia, and a legend belonging particularly to what is now the diocese of Kootenay. Born in Ireland in 1859, the son of a Church of Ireland clergyman, Henry Irwin went to Keble College, Oxford, and received his degree in 1881. After serving a curacy at Rugby he offered himself for missionary service abroad. How he came to decide upon British Columbia as a sphere of work is not known except that from boyhood he had affirmed that he was going to be a missionary, and in a country with a cold climate.

He came to British Columbia in 1885, and after two years at Kamloops moved to Donald, high up in the mountains, where he remained until 1890. For those who know Donald today, a ghost of its former self, it may be difficult to realise that in Father Pat's day it was a hive of industry with more than a thousand men in the vicinity. In many respects these were, with the exception of his short married life in New Westminster, the happiest days of his life. During his tenure at Donald, Father Pat became engaged to Frances Stuart Innes, a sister of Mrs. Shildrick. The couple were married at the beginning of 1890 and settled down in New Westminster where Irwin had been appointed chaplain to the bishop and assistant curate at Holy Trinity Cathedral. Their happiness was short-lived, however, for Mrs. Irwin died in childbirth before the end of the year. It is probably because of these circumstances that from this time forward Father Pat became increasingly determined to work in rough and isolated places.

While in Donald he had commended himself to all, and not least to the men at work on the construction of the Canadan Pacific Railway. There was no church in Donald when Irwin went there and services were held in the Court House. At first, only the women came, for, as one writer has remarked, "religion seems to form but a small part of the life of male colonists, even those who have been accustomed to fulfill its duties in the home country."[1] Slowly he won his way not only by his unflagging faithfulness as a parish priest but also by his affection and concern for his people as their friend.

One incident in which this was quickly brought out was connected with a snowslide in which a railwayman from Donald had lost his life. As soon as the news of the slide and its consequences were known, the superintendent and other men went out to clear the line. The snow was still coming down in small slides and there was no communication between these men and the station in Donald. Mrs. Green, the wife of the dead railwayman, was beside herself with grief and anxiety, frantic lest nothing be done to recover her husband's body. Quietly, Father Pat slipped away from Donald with a small toboggan which could move over the snow where an engine could not cut its way through. Taking no notice of the threatening snowslides, he made his way to where the dead man lay. Reverently he wrapped the body and placed it on the toboggan and made his way back to Donald. He was away two days and a night, including a night spent alone with the dead man on the desolate and dangerous road.

Before long a church was built in Donald, and the story was thus told in the Kamloops paper:

> A short time ago the Church people determined to have a Church; a large congregation having been collected by the indefatigable exertions of the Rev. F. [sic] Irwin, applications were made to all persons who were thought likely to assist in the good work; the C.P.R. gave a site and other assistance; collections were taken up; articles of furniture promised, and such a general interest taken in the work that the result was soon apparent. In a few short weeks a really church-like building was erected, well finished, and opened for the worship of Almighty God according to the Faith of the English Church. This Church at Donald has the honor of being the first church of any kind built within the range of the rockies.[2]

The church was given the name St. Peter's.

Father Pat was not content, however, to remain even at comparative ease in Donald. A few weeks after the opening of the Church he heard that "mountain fever was raging among the North West Mounted Police"[3] who were camped below Wild Horse Creek near the Tobacco Plains. This, together with the fact that there were a number of men at work on the preparations for the cutting of a canal to drain the Kootenay river into the Columbia lakes, made him feel that a trip through the district was absolutely necessary. Because it was too late to undertake the journey by steamer from Golden to the Columbia lakes, and thence by the wagon road, he made it, instead, from what he described as "the hurricane deck of a cayuse"[4] and a rough trip it was, taking three days. Services were held, the sick cared for, and settlers visited along the way, and all were anxious for the regular ministrations of the Church "and the kind of support which took the form of a subscription in the N.W.M.P. camp 'for the support of the Church of England missions in the Kootenay district', proved that this desire is more than a nominal one, by giving $43 towards our mission.'[5] After the service in one of the barrack rooms he held services for some of the settlers, and then on the Sunday was able to have a celebration of Holy Communion before riding thirty miles for Evensong at Windermere.

At the beginning of 1888, Father Pat returned to Ireland for family reasons and little more was done in the Kootenays for the time being. Meanwhile, the population was growing because of mining discoveries and at the end of 1891 Bishop Sillitoe wrote in his annual report:

> Nelson, our important mining centre, though geographically within the Kamloops District, is beyond the reach of any one of the three Priests employed there, and must be dealt with independently. The S.P.G. voted a grant of £100 a year, for two years, for a Mission there, but it is necessary that the balance of the stipend should be made up before we send a man in. An effort is being made in England now in this direction, which I hope will shortly be successful, and enable us to take possession of the field before the summer.[6]

The Bishop's hopes were realised and in May he was able to accompany the Reverend A. J. Reid to Nelson and there to introduce him to the congregation as priest-in-charge of the newly formed Kootenay Missionary District. Within a few months a building had been completed which could be used both as a Mission Chapel and a reading room, but times were bad and mining prospects poor. The Sunday collections had dropped from twenty dollars to four. Whether the prospects were altogether too gloomy for Reid is not clear but within a year he had resigned the mission and returned to the diocese of Toronto. His place was taken by the Reverend H. S. Akehurst, Vicar of St. Peter's Pro-Cathedral, Qu'Appelle, who was to spend the rest of his life in British Columbia, and become the first Archdeacon of Kamloops.

In 1896 Father Pat, who had again been in Ireland, returned to New Westminster and was appointed by Bishop Dart as Mission Priest at Rossland, then a rapidly growing mining district in the mountains. While in Rossland, he ministered to all and sundry, claiming the acquaintance of every soul he met, giving away his means and his clothes and sharing his living accommodation with sick and homeless miners. At first, there being no church, a building grandly known as the Opera House, was rented for services. Soon, however, land was secured and St. George's Church was built. A church, dedicated to St. Andrew, was also built in Trail, six miles away, at the foot of the mountain.

Once again his activities were not confined to his immediate environment. Trail, Grand Forks, Boundary, Kettle Valley were all familiar places, and, as well, he held the licence of the Bishop of Spokane enabling him to officiate in communities across the line in the State of Washington. It delighted him to show that "the forty-ninth parallel doesn't run through the church, even if it's found in Custom Houses."[7] Nor were all his undertakings strictly pastoral for one well known story tells how

a prospector lay sick away out on the lonely mountainside, thirty miles from doctor or medicine. Father Pat heard of it. He gathered together medicines, and hit the trail. While nearing the cabin, he came across three mounted miners who saluted him with the question, "Hello, parson, where are you going?" He told them. "Bill needs a doctor instead of a parson!" They commenced to abuse the minister. They would not let him pass. Quicker than lightning the parson jerked one of the miners off his horse, knocked another one off, and cleared the trail.

He reached the sick man's side, and ministered to his wants. On returning next day he met the three miners, who had camped on the trail bent on revenge. While being abused he appeared as meek as a lamb. The trio surrounded him in a threatening manner. Then the parson spoke: "Will you see fair play if I fight one at a time?"

said he. "Yes, yes, yes," exclaimed they, chuckling with delight at the prospect.

A ring was formed, and soon one of the three measured his length on the ground. "Come on," said Father Pat pleasantly, as the other two seemed somewhat dazed. One came on, and followed the first. "Next," said Father Pat, but the third miner took to his heels as though his Satanic Majesty was behind him instead of only a meek minister. The Father bathed the bruises of the two prostrate figures and after preaching them a sermon on the iniquity of fighting, went on his way.[8]

It was apparent to the Bishop, however, that Father Pat was wearing himself out and he offered him an easier, lighter post, but Irwin begged to be sent out as a pioneer, and at last had his way by being transferred, in 1900, to Fairview in the southern Okanagan. Fairview, in those days, was a flourishing community west of the present town of Oliver. It has since disappeared. Irwin's strength was failing and the Bishop urged him to take a rest, to go home for a time to Ireland, to visit his friends, and then to come back should he wish to do so. Evidently, Father Pat agreed on condition that when he returned to British Columbia he should undertake work as an itinerant missionary to isolated settlers.

What happened thereafter no one quite knows. Irwin set off for England at the end of 1901 and it is surmised that he left the train some distance before it reached Montreal, intending to walk on. Some time later he was picked up by a farmer and taken to the Notre Dame Hospital in Montreal where his feet were found to be so badly frozen that his boots had to be cut from them. He would not say anything about himself, nor give any other name than William Henry, but to Dr. Kingston, the house doctor, he committed his papers and letters to friends pledging him to complete secrecy until after his death. As soon as the Sisters who maintained the hospital learned that their mysterious patient was an

Anglican they sent for Father Wood, rector of St. John's Church, Montreal, who ministered to him for the few days before he died. Towards morning, on January 13th, 1902, he lost consciousness, and died a little before midday, without having regained his senses. His body was brought back to Sapperton and there buried alongside those of his wife and tiny child.

The church at Donald which Father Pat had built was, like its founder, destined to have an unusual end, since it was moved a few years later to Windermere—a distance of about one hundred miles. The reason for the move was the transfer of the Canadian Pacific Railway Company's repair shops to Revelstoke. As these were almost the only source of employment and income the village of Donald was practically annihilated. The collapse of Donald and the removal of its church has given rise to the legend of the stolen church, which runs somewhat as follows.

When the failure of Donald occurred the church was also to be moved to Revelstoke, a proceeding which the few remaining inhabitants of Donald bitterly opposed. A crew was recruited to dismantle the church and transport it to its new site, but when they arrived the building had disappeared and no one would give any hint of what had happened to it. Later, it appeared that one of the parishioners in Donald, Rufus A. Kimpton, who had done a great deal of work on the church, had a part interest in two stores, one in Donald and the other in Windermere. Since his future interests were now to be in Windermere it seemed to him logical enough that the church should be taken there also. He, therefore, with the support of some of his friends who wished the church to go anywhere rather than Revelstoke, had it dismantled and loaded on to flat cars to be taken by rail to Golden, whence it was shipped by barge to Windermere and rebuilt. The scheme worked perfectly, much to the consternation of the church people of Revelstoke. But there was one hitch. The church at Donald had possessed a bell, which had been given by the Baroness Burdett-Coutts, but when the structure arrived at Windermere the bell was missing. It later transpired that the manager of the river barge company which took the building from Golden to Windermere was a parishioner of St. Paul's, Golden, and thought that the bell would grace his own church. Since the church was being stolen in the first place he saw no reason why he should not help himself to the bell for this purpose. Thus the parish-ioners of Windermere worship Sunday by Sunday in a stolen church while their fellows at Golden are summoned to service by a stolen bell.

Such is the legend and pleasant though it is there are some difficulties connected with it: first, there seems to be little or no documentary evidence to support it; second, Revelstoke already had a church built in 1896, and enlarged by the addition of a chancel just before the exodus from Donald in the summer of 1899;[9] third, the proposal to take the church to Windermere was being considered by the diocesan authorities as early as March, 1899;[10] and lastly, in August of the same year it was reported that "arrangements had been concluded with the consent of the Vicar and Church officials for the removal of Donald's church fabric to Windermere, *the bell and furniture remaining at the disposal of the Vicar and officials of the Donald and Golden parishes.*"[11] The one slight piece of evidence in support of the legend is the reference to some letters which seem to be no longer extant from the Reverend H. B. Turner, Vicar of Golden and Donald, protesting against the removal of the building to Win-dermere apparently on the grounds that he was not completely informed of what was happening.[12]

The fate of the church in Donald is an example of the extra-ordinary fluidity of populations and towns in early pioneer days not only in British Columbia, but in western Canada as a whole. Donald, Fairview, Fort Steele, Douglas and Phoenix are all examples of communities which have flourished for a time and then disappeared or shrunk to a shadow of their former size. In the Kootenays the influx was drawn by the prospect of fortunes to be made in mining copper, zinc, lead, silver, or coal. Often this influx was followed by a real estate boom which, as a rule, profited no one but the unscrupulous land sharks. Then, not infrequently, the early promise failed and the self-styled towns and cities wilted overnight. Another factor in these rises and declines was to be found in the development of railways and, later, of roads which sometimes passed by this or that community leaving it to perish in isolation while a new community sprang up in a more favoured site.

Reference has already been made to Father Pat's journey to Fort Steele out of which grew the Kootenay Missionary district with headquarters at Nelson. A few years later the Reverend C. A. Procunier, who had formerly been a Methodist minister in Edmonton, was ordained and appointed to Fort Steele; this proved to be but a passing phase for when he left to go to Revelstoke in 1900 no successor was placed there—the next appointment being to Cranbrook which by then overshadowed Fort Steele. Fort Steele continued to languish for some years always hoping that there might sometime be a resurgence of life. The completion of the Kootenay Central Railway in 1911 seemed to give promise of better things but in 1913 it was still sadly recorded that "Fort Steele is . . . unoccupied. . . . There is a nice vicarage and also a building that has been used for some years as a church, though not at all attractive in appearance, nor suitable in its arrangements. The people have the money in hand for a nice church building and are only waiting the appointment of an energetic Incumbent before undertaking to build."[13] But the population continued to dwindle, the "energetic Incumbent" was never appointed, and the church never built.

Cranbrook, on the other hand, flourished mightily. To the parish in 1901 came the Reverend Havelock Beacham, B.A., of St. John's College, Winnipeg, and a church was built which soon proved to be too small. In 1914 the rector, the Reverend E. P. Flewelling, reported that the church in Cranbrook was "playing a losing game, because of the lack of proper seating accommodations. Frequently people come for services and then go away from the Church door because there is not room for them."[14] At Creston, beyond Cranbrook, services were held as early as 1899, a resident clergyman appointed in 1909 in the person of the Reverend P. C. Hayman, and a church built two years later.

Eastward from Cranbrook in the growing town of Fernie, services were first held in the Bank of Commerce building in 1898 and a church built with no external financial aid in the following year. The Reverend W. H. Hedley, B.A., who had worked among the Durham miners in England, was appointed to the parish in 1900. Few parishes, however, can have had a more tragic history than Fernie. In 1902 there was a mine explosion which killed 130 men bringing sorrow and distress to many homes. Two years later the town was swept by fire destroying the church and rectory among many other buildings. Both were rebuilt but in 1908 forest fires roared through the Crow's Nest Pass destroying Fernie, Hosmer, and Michel. Once again the church and rectory were destroyed along with the homes of nearly all the parishioners, but with courage the congregation began anew. First came a cement basement in which the services were held for a year or two, and then on Christmas Day, 1911, services were held for the first time in the fine new brick church.[15] A mission was also established at Michel and Morrissey further up the Crow's Nest Pass under the guidance of the Reverend Ackroyd Stoney, another ex-Methodist minister who was ordained by Bishop Dart.

In the western Kootenays were the parishes of Greenwood and Phoenix. In the former a church was erected dedicated to St. Jude, and the work waxed and then waned in the familiar pattern leaving a community which was but a ghost of its former self. Phoenix came into being as a mining town in 1899 and two years later the Reverend E. P. Flewelling became the vicar. With a population of 1300, even though it was divided into six congregations, the future was promising.[16] But the slump came. The church struggled on, more often than not without a resident priest, and finally both church and community disappeared.

All this may suggest a weak and unsatisfactory missionary programme in which progress seemed impossible. Certainly, it was discouraging for those immediately involved, and boded ill for the future. Yet, as we have suggested, it was but a stage in the development of a new country. As time passed lines of communication became clearly defined, the economy more stable and communities more firmly established. In this second stage the Church was received and respected as a pioneer among pioneers, and, profiting from the vicissitudes and experiences of the past, was able to expand her work in new and rising permanent centres.

---

1 Mrs. Jerome Mercier, *Father Pat*, Minchin and Gibbs, Gloucester, 1909, p.45. Much of the earlier part of this chapter is drawn from this book.
2 *Inland Sentinel*, September 17th, 1887.
3 *Churchman's Gazette*, December, 1887, pp.461-2.
4 *Ibid.*
5 *Ibid.*
6 *Churchman's Gazette*, February, 1892, p.894.
7 Mercier, op. cit., p.90.
8 Mercier, op. cit., p.87.
9 *Work for the Far West*, October, 1899, p.22.

10 Minutes, Executive Committee of the Synod of the Diocese of New Westminster, March 8th, 1899.
11 Minutes, Executive Committee of the Synod of the Diocese of New Westminster, August 2nd, 1899. (Author's italics.)
12 Minutes, Executive Committee of the Synod of the Diocese of New Westminster, May 25th, 1899.
13 British Columbia and Yukon Church Aid Society, *Year Book*, 1914, p.214.
14 *Ibid.*, p.212.
15 British Columbia Church Aid Society, *Year Book*, 1911, p.48.
16 *Work for the Far West*, January, 1902, p.26.

# 11

# Marine Missions

IT WAS not long after the establishment of the Crown Colony of British Columbia that the possibilities of Burrard Inlet for commercial shipping became apparent. "As early as 1863," wrote Judge Howay, "G. Tranfield, a fish and game dealer in New Westminster, sent several men to the inlet to fish for cod to supply the markets of the mainland. John Robson, the owner and editor of the *British Columbian*, . . . urged capitalists to canvass carefully the possibilities of this industry. In that connection he stressed the necessity for a road from New Westminster that should reach the inlet near the First Narrows. He had already pointed to the timber wealth, . . ."[1]

It was this timber wealth which attracted deep-sea shipping and in November, 1864, the first shipment of lumber left for Australia. The completion of the Canadian Pacific Railway in

1887 saw the establishment of Vancouver as one of the deep-sea ports of the world. A seaport is necessarily a cosmopolitan centre with sailors coming and going from many lands. Loading was a slow process and sometimes a ship would be in port for two or three months at a time during which period the seamen were thrown on their own resources. The only recreation provided for them was that afforded by the saloons along Water Street.

Soon after the arrival of the Reverend H. G. Fiennes-Clinton at St. James' Church, Granville, as it was then, he realised the need for a sailors' social and recreational centre, and opened a building adjoining the church as a Seamen's Institute. The date of its opening is unknown, but in the *Vancouver Directory* for 1897-98 it is listed as follows:

> Seamen's Institute, Gore Ave.,
> reading and recreation rooms;
> open every evening.
> President: Rev. H. G. F. Clinton,
> Sec'y: C. T. Sayce.

At the beginning of the present century it was realised that the responsibility for such an institution was more than parochial and the Executive Committee of the Diocese of New Westminster agreed, in 1903, "that the monthly sum of $10 should be paid to the Rev. H. G. F. Clinton in aid of the Vancouver Seamen's Mission under his superintendence."[2] Shortly after this, in 1904, the institute became part of an English society, the Missions to Seamen, known throughout the world as the Flying Angel Mission. As the port and the new city grew in size and importance the original buildings became too small and a move was made to the West End. In 1922 fire forced another move, this time to 1121 Hastings Street, then known as Seaton Street. In this building, which had originally been the home of Dr. Henry Bell-Irving, the work of the mission was carried on for thirty-four years until a new building was opened in 1954. Branches of the Missions to Seamen were also opened at New Westminster in 1929, and at North Vancouver in 1935.

Not only did logging operations develop in the vicinity of Vancouver but they also spread along the coast. Settlers moved in and soon many communities were established in isolated places on the mainland and among the islands. It was natural that the presence of such settlements and their needs should be particularly apparent to Father Clinton whose work at St. James' and at the Seamen's Institute brought him into contact with loggers and settlers as they came into Vancouver. At a meeting of the Executive Committee of the Diocese of New Westminster early in 1904 he "brought up the matter of ministrations to the settlers on the coast," and said that "he had had communications from people as far up as Namu stating their needs."[3] The matter was discussed and the suggestion made that the work could best be done by a steam yacht which would serve as a travelling mission church. It would also be wise, it was pointed out, to collaborate with the Diocese of British Columbia which had jurisdiction over the islands. The idea was not a new one since Bishop Ridley had used the steam yacht *Evangeline* in northern waters as early as 1880, and by 1884 the Methodists had established a marine mission under the superintendence of the Reverend Thomas Crosby.

A committee was appointed consisting of Archdeacon Pentreath, Father Clinton, and the Reverend John Antle to investigate the need and to consult with the authorities of the Diocese of British Columbia. The latter agreed that action should be taken and it was decided that the Reverend John Antle should spend the month of June, 1904, looking over the ground after which he would present recommendations for possible action. Antle was a Newfoundlander, born to the sea, who had come to

Vancouver in 1900, to take charge of the newly established parish of Holy Trinity, Fairview district, Vancouver. During his stay in Vancouver he had built a small fourteen-foot boat which he called *Laverock,* and in this vessel accompanied by his son, he sailed as far as Alert Bay visiting settlements and logging camps en route. He returned with the conviction that action should be taken at once. "Saloons were [being] built before the camps, but the Church was slow to follow: Sunday was a drunken carousal. The work to be a success must have a social side to it, reading rooms, libraries, etc., were a necessity. Within a year Mr. Antle believed the work might be self-supporting, the men promised active support, . . ."4 The matter was further discussed and agreement reached on the urgent need for action. The cost of a suitable vessel would be $3,500 and it was decided that the Diocese of New Westminster should provide half the cost on the understanding that British Columbia would raise the other half. The Missionary Society of the Church in Canada was also to be approached for assistance.

By the end of 1904 the funds had been raised and in the following year the Mission Ship *Columbia* was built at Wallace's Shipyards, Vancouver. It was sixty-five feet long and its cabin quarters included a small hospital and a chapel. The Reverend John Antle was appointed as Superintendent of the Columbia Coast Mission. But as Antle pointed out, more than preaching was required. One of the most pressing needs was for medical service. To illustrate this he cited the instance of Oscar Soderman, a logger on Minstrel Island, whose closest friend had been crushed by a falling tree, sustaining two broken legs and several broken ribs. Soderman followed the routine procedure. He rowed his friend out to sea in on open boat and tried to dull his agony with copious draughts of whiskey. For forty-eight hours Soderman kept a lookout for passing vessels. Finally he was able to attract the attention of a vessel bound for Vancouver. The injured logger was lifted aboard but gangrene had set in during the long wait in the open boat. In Vancouver both his legs had to be amputated. "In conditions like that," said Antle, "it's no good going up to the logger and preaching. We must demonstrate our Christianity with deeds."[5]

In order to meet such needs as this, a small hospital was built with the support of the Hastings Mill Company, at Rock Bay, one hundred and thirty miles north of Vancouver. The nursing staff was provided by the Victorian Order of Nurses. The hospital was opened by Archdeacon Pentreath who expressed himself as being gratified by the progress of the new venture. Moreover, he felt that within a year the mission would be self-supporting and no longer in need of diocesan grants in aid of the superintendent's stipend. Within five years grants from the provincial government and the Missionary Society of the Church in Canada together with private donations enabled the Mission to put three ships on patrol. In 1908 a meeting was held at Alert Bay which asked the Mission to consider the erection of a hospital there for the Indian and white inhabitants of the area. Among those present was the Reverend A. J. Hall who had come as a C.M.S. missionary in 1878, and who added his warm support to the proposal. John Antle, with his usual courage, began to make plans and on June 15th, 1909, the first St. George's Hospital was opened and dedicated by Bishop Perrin of British Columbia.

It soon became apparent that a larger vessel was needed for the work that the *Columbia* was called upon to do and in 1909 Antle went to England to raise the necessary funds. He had almost completed arrangements for the purchase of a 107 foot vessel built in England when he discovered that it would cost a prodigious sum to bring it to the Pacific coast. He cancelled the transaction and instead ordered a 100 foot ship which was designed and built in New Westminster. This second *Columbia* was dedicated in Victoria in 1910. Twenty-two years later when this ship was due for replacement Antle heard of one for sale in Monte Carlo. The British Columbia and Yukon Church Aid Society bought her for the Mission and she was dedicated at Lambeth Pier on June 13th, 1933, by the Right Reverend A. F. Winington-Ingram, Lord Bishop of London. Antle himself, with the aid of five volunteers, sailed her to Vancouver by way of the Azores and the Panama Canal.

During the years that followed the Columbia Coast Mission built twelve churches and three hospitals, and by 1936 had 45 agents, the majority being chaplains, doctors, nurses, and lay-readers.

Reference has already been made to Bishop Ridley's little steamer, the *Evangeline*, which he used for missionary work along the coast and among the islands of his diocese. After twelve years, however, the Bishop found that the cost of maintaining her was too great and the vessel was sold. He then spent the winter of 1892-93 in England seeking to recover his health which had been gravely impaired by the perils and hardships to which he had been exposed. On his return he wrote sadly to the S.P.G.,

> Because I have been unfit to buffet with storms, I have not attempted to use my open boat in visitation, but did the best I could by taking my chances on the trading vessels that ply on these waters. My own diocesan steamer, my *Evangeline*, I was forced—shall I confess the truth?—by poverty to sell. Could I have kept her, I should, I think, be hale now instead of an invalid. I had to choose between the extension of the Gospel, and a safe and expeditious means of keeping in touch with our work and workers that has cost me from £200 to £400 per annum, and with occasional costly repairs sometimes exceeding my income.[6]

For the next twenty years reliance had to be placed on open boats and canoes, but in 1912, encouraged no doubt by the success of the Columbia Coast Mission, a further attempt was made to establish a marine mission in northern waters. In 1905, the Reverend Walter Field Rushbrook, B.A., had come from Ontario to take charge of Port Essington. After a few years he, too, realised the need of a mission ship, and with £100 given him by the Navvy Society for his services among the men who worked on the construction of the Grand Trunk Pacific Railway, he bought a small motor launch, the *Fern S*, with which he was able to visit the railway construction camps along the coast and up the Skeena river. Finding that the boat was inadequate against the strong currents, Rushbrook prevailed upon Bishop Du Vernet to build a more powerful vessel, and so the *Northern Cross*, a 45-foot motor launch, was built and commissioned in the fall of 1912.

The *Northern Cross* continued in service for many years serving an increasing number of logging camps, fisheries, and isolated settlements. Rushbrook was made an Honorary Canon of Prince Rupert Cathedral in 1922, and continued as superintendent of the Prince Rupert Coast Mission until 1928 when he was succeeded by the Reverend W. Bruce Jennings, who afterwards became Dean of Algoma. About the same time it was discovered that the *Northern Cross* would soon need to be replaced, and a new ship was built in 1931 at a cost of $15,000, of which $10,000 came as a gift from an anonymous friend in England. The work continued and in 1933 Jennings was succeeded by the Reverend William Alexander Delap. Captain Delap was a master mariner who had entered the Sacred Ministry. After training at the Theological College in Vancouver, he was ordained by Bishop Rix and appointed to Telegraph Creek, but with the vacancy on the *Northern Cross* he returned to the sea, there to serve until 1937, when he retired to Ireland.

As the work along the coast expanded it became apparent that a second vessel was required and in 1914, James Gillett, a student of Wycliffe College, Toronto, was ordained for missionary work in the vicinity of Porcher Island. In 1915 the *Western Hope* was built and put into service. Her home port was at Massett on the Queen Charlotte Islands where the work had been begun by Archdeacon Collison forty years earlier. After a number of years of service Gillett was appointed Indian Agent at Massett and was succeeded on the *Western Hope*, first by the Reverend C. O. Darby, of Emmanuel College, Saskatoon, and then, in 1929, by the Reverend R. P. Graham, who came to the mission from the Diocese of Brandon.

---

1 F. W. Howay, "Early Shipping in Burrard Inlet, 1863-70", *B. C. Historical Quarterly*, Vol. 1, No. 1, Jan. 1937, pp.3-20.

2 Minutes of the Executive Committee, Synod of the Diocese of New Westminster, May 13th, 1903.

3 Minutes of the Executive Committee, Synod of the Diocese of New Westminster, March 16th, 1904.

4 Minutes of the Executive Committee, Synod of the Diocese of New Westminster, August 17th, 1904.

5 *British Columbia Marine Missions*, unpublished essay by the Reverend E. D. Powell, B.A., Anglican Theological College, Vancouver, 1958.

6 Alice J. Janvrin (Ed.), *Snapshots from the North Pacific*, C.M.S., London, 1904, p.76.

# 12

# Missions to
# Orientals

AMONG the many who came to British Columbia with
the 1858 discovery of gold were a few Chinese. They had been
sent by their compatriots to examine the situation and report on
the possibilities of success. The result was that many hundreds
of Chinese made their way to the gold diggings. Judge Howay
points out that having arrived,

> as the white miners left bar after bar on the lower Fraser where good
> wages could be made, to follow the latest, but often untrue and
> always exaggerated rumours of richer diggings in more inaccessible
> spots, [the Chinese] took up the abandoned ground, and toiled
> patiently and diligently thereon until the returns dwindled to the
> vanishing point. This is the story of mining: the white miner never
> content, always working with both ears open to catch the first vague
> whisper of richer ground to be found just under the fringe of the
> unknown, ever ready to abandon the substance for the shadow, the
> Chinese content, immovable, deaf to such rumours, clinging tena-
> ciously to his ground so long as it continued to yield the least profit.[1]

By 1863, it was estimated that there were 2,500 Chinese in British Columbia[2] and the Church was not slow to realise the importance of missionary work amongst them.

Bishop Hills had not long been in his new diocese when he realised the needs and possibilities of such work. In Victoria, he reported that there were many Chinese, and among them Quong Hing who had given £10 towards the new St. John's Church. The Bishop hoped that this augured well for the future. In New Westminster, the Reverend John Sheepshanks had several Chinese under regular instruction,[3] while in Yale, centre of the mining community, there were large numbers of Chinese, ten of whom contributed to the building of the church there. At Yale, too, the Church was fortunate in having Henry Reeve, a lay missionary, who had formerly worked in China, and was able to converse with the Chinese in their own tongue. In fact, he said, he looked to the Chinese and Indian work with more encouragement than that of the white population.[4]

By 1866 Chinese had penetrated the Cariboo, partly to search for gold, but also to work as merchants, farmers, servants and labourers. At Quesnel, the Reverend A. C. Garrett visited a farm belonging to some Chinese and was "delighted and inspired by the skill and success with which they worked, and also by their ingenuity in securing water for irrigation."[5] The Chinese, however, were not particularly interested in receiving Christian missionaries, and shortly after moving to Lytton, the Reverend J. B. Good commented that although willing enough to avail themselves of secular training and instruction "the Chinese population inhabiting this Colony wholly keep aloof from our influence, and have not apparently even the curiosity or interest to enquire concerning our holy faith and practice."[6]

Evangelistic efforts continued, however, and in the late 1880's or early 1890's a Chinese lay catechist named S. Ten Yong, who had worked in Honolulu, was working among the Chinese both in Victoria and New Westminster. In 1892, a night school for Chinese men and boys was begun in New Westminster by the Reverend H. H. Gowen, who had gone from St. Augustine's College, Canterbury, to serve as missionary to the Chinese in Honolulu, and had come to British Columbia earlier in the year.[7] The school had the blessing and support of the Canadian Church Missionary Society, and quickly increased in numbers. Before long a similar school was opened at Christ Church, Vancouver, and a Chinese Mission Aid Association[8] was formed to support Chinese work in the diocese. A room on Pender Street, Vancouver, was obtained for the school which had the support of the clergy of Christ Church and St. Paul's as well as of a number of enthusiastic women.

The fruits of the mission began to appear when on September 25th, 1893, six Chinese men were baptized in Christ Church, Vancouver, by the Reverend H. H. Gowen, in the presence of a number of their own people as well as of the white congregation.[9] At the same time it was decided to move to larger premises, still on Pender Street, but where it would be possible to have a reading room and sitting room, chapel, kitchen, and rooms for a dozen or so men to live in in order that they might remain in a Christian environment during their early days in the Faith.

The Reverend L. N. Tucker, M.A., who became rector of Christ Church, Vancouver, in 1894, was a man of keen missionary spirit, and fully aware of the importance of the Chinese mission which had been established in his parish. In 1900 he presented a report[10] urging the appointment of a Chinese-speaking priest to be assisted by an adequate number of Chinese catechists in the larger centres of population. Such work could not be carried on without funds and he thought that at least $2,000 per annum would be required. He felt that in 1901, when the thankoffering of the Women's Auxiliary of the ecclesiastical province of Canada was to be devoted to the Chinese of British Columbia "a determined effort should be made to erect a building that would be a permanent centre of the work, and answer the varied purposes of a chapel for worship, a schoolroom for secular and religious teaching, and a lodging house for the catechists and converts.[11]

As a result of this appeal a building on Homer Street was secured and opened on January 22nd, 1903. It proved impossible to find a Chinese clergyman and the work was entrusted to James Hall, (Anglicised form of Hau), a Chinese catechist, under the supervision of the Reverend C. C. Owen, B.A., who had now become rector of Christ Church, and a Chinese Mission Committee. For a time the work went well enough. The school was open five evenings a week with an average attendance of thirty-five Chinese pupils and four volunteer teachers. On Sunday the Christian Chinese and those under instruction attended Christ Church in the morning, and took part in services at the mission, conducted by Hall, in the afternoon and evening. In addition, the catechist visited the Chinese homes in the area, and made an annual trip to the canneries where many of the Chinese were employed during the summer. As time went on it became apparent that Hall was not very satisfactory and that perhaps the mission was not near enough to the centre of Chinatown. In 1907 Hall was released from his appointment and his place taken by George Lim Yuen who had, for some time previously, been doing part of the work on a voluntary basis. Lim Yuen was admitted to the diaconate on Trinity Sunday, 1914, by Bishop de Pencier after a period of training at Latimer Hall, and ordained to the priesthood in 1920. At the beginning of 1917, the Reverend Neville Lascalles Ward, M.A., who had been a missionary of the M.S.C.C. in Honan, China, was appointed Superintendent of the Chinese Mission, with the continuing assistance of Lim Yuen.

The work in New Westminster during this period was in abeyance owing to lack of a catechist. The Reverend H. H. Gowen had moved to Trinity Church, Seattle, in 1897, and after his departure there was no one to keep the Chinese work alive. Soon after Bishop Dart's arrival the Chinese classes were resumed at the see house as there was no other accommodation. James Hall acted for a time as catechist until the Bishop moved him to Vancouver when James Chou was appointed. Chou was a young Chinese whom the Bishop had baptized and confirmed some four years previously. In 1900, a quarter section farm in the vicinity of Hammond was given to the diocese for the benefit of Chinese work in New Westminster by Mrs. Greswolde Williams, of Acton, London. It was later divided into 20 acre lots and sold to provide funds for a Chinese Mission building.[12]

Japanese immigration to British Columbia began later than the Chinese, but by 1907 the Japanese were arriving in large numbers and attempts were being made to secure the passage of legislation to exclude them.[13] As they arrived they made their way into sawmills, the fishing industry, farming and to a lesser degree into other occupations. Bishop Dart of New Westminster pointed out to his Synod in 1900[14] that as the orientals arrived they should be treated with "kindly consideration, equity, and justice,"[15] and that steps should be taken to preach the Gospel among them. A few years later, in 1904, Archdeacon Pentreath reported that a school had been started for them in the Flack Block, Vancouver, by Kathleen O'Melia. There were at the time twenty students and their progress was encouraging.[16] At the same time a Japanese Mission Committee was set up and Gabriel Yosen Fujita, a highly respected Christian Japanese, was appointed stipendiary catechist. The Woman's Auxiliary has always been active in supporting the work, and at this time St. James' branch contributed twenty dollars, no small sum in those days, which paid for prayer and hymn books, and helped towards the rent of the schoolroom.[17] In the following year a Japanese Mission House was built on East Cordova Street at a cost of $4,500, to which the Japanese themselves contributed $357. Soon a number of catechumens were baptized and confirmed. One of them, Bernard F. Oana, was later to be ordained and appointed superintendent of the Japanese Mission.

By 1909, the number of Japanese in British Columbia was increasing and the population, which had consisted almost entirely of men, was being augmented by the arrival of women and children. A Japanese Mission Committee of the New Westminster Diocesan W. A. was formed and a second mission opened on West Second Avenue in the Holy Trinity parish. Mrs. F. W. Patrick, a certificated teacher who had had some experience with orientals, was asked to undertake the work. Her salary was paid by the W. A. while individual parishes made themselves responsible for the maintenance of the mission premises.

The mission opened in a second floor room on June 14th, 1909, with an ungraded day school for the children and sewing and reading classes for the women. There was also a Sunday School of about 21 pupils. In the following November nine catechumens were baptized so, despite opposition from the Buddhists, it could be felt that progress was being made.

Mrs. Patrick records an amusing incident concerning George, an Indian boy from the Nass River, who had been attracted to the Mission. George evidently liked to sing, and among the hymns he had learned was one called, "Bringing in the Sheaves." This, he suggested, should now be taught to the little Japanese. What was Mrs. Patrick's consternation, however, when a little later she heard her charges singing:

"We will come to Georgie,
Bringing in the cheese."

The work continued to increase and soon consideration was being given to the erection of a new building towards which $300 had been contributed by the Japanese, and $2,000 given by the W.A.[18] The house at 1622 West Second Avenue was opened on March 30th, 1912, and later became known as the Mission of the Ascension.

Meanwhile, the work at Cordova Street continued to flourish with the support and interest of St. James' Church. In 1911, the Reverend H. G. Fynes-Clinton,[19] chairman of the supervisory committee, reported that

> the numbers daily attending for instruction have increased, and the interest taken by the students in the Christian religion, judging from outward appearance, is very encouraging . . . . Whether there will be many conversions as the result is, of course, not for us to say. We can only sow the seed, and leave the results. But one would fain hope that the Holy Spirit is working in the hearts of those who hear, and that their wills may be bent to accept the faith is the constant hope and prayer of those engaged in the work of the Mission.
>
> Lately there has been a movement among the Japanese to collect money for the stipend of a Japanese priest, and there are some thirty dollars promised monthly for [his] stipend from the Japanese Christians and students. I have been corresponding with the Bishops in Japan with the hope of obtaining a priest for the work; but hitherto without success.[20]

In 1913, the Japanese Mission faced a major crisis precipitated by the defection of Miss O'Melia and her helpers and followers to the Church of Rome. This seems to be the beginning of Roman Catholic missions to the Japanese in Canada, and the incident placed the infant Anglican Japanese Mission in Vancouver in embarrassing circumstances for the time being. In spite of the handicap the mission continued to make progress under its new missionary, Miss Porter, who was now assisted by Bernard

The 'stolen church' at
Windermere, about 1900.

Reverend Henry Irwin
(Father Pat)

*Reverend John Antle*

*The mission ship* Columbia.

Oana who had become a student at St. Mark's Hall. It was still felt, however, that the great need was for a priest who could minister to the Japanese in their own tongue. Such a man was found in the person of the Reverend F. W. Cassilis Kennedy, M.A., a graduate of Trinity College, Toronto, who had spent most of his ministry in Japan, and who came to Vancouver to be Superintendent of the Japanese Mission at the end of 1914.

As the work grew the need for consolidation became apparent and in 1915 a composite Oriental Missions Committee was set up with representatives from the Synod and from the Diocesan Board of the W.A. At the same time it was felt that because of the scattered nature of the work throughout the province an extra-diocesan agency was required. A Memorial was therefore addressed to General Synod[21] urging that body "to take into consideration this whole question," and suggesting "that the M.S.C.C. should take over, become responsible for, and carry on this as one of its departments of work." The memorial was also presented to the newly-formed Provincial Synod of British Columbia in 1917[22] and resulted in the adoption of a Canon setting up the Provincial Board of Missions to Orientals.

Before passing on to discuss the work done under the auspices of this new board there remains one other aspect of earlier oriental work, namely the ministry to the East Indians. The first contingent of East Indians, forty-five in number, arrived in 1905 but within a few years there were several thousand of them resident in British Columbia.[23] They worked for the most part as unskilled labourers in the sawmills, and to a lesser degree in dairying and farming both on Vancouver Island and in the vicinity of Vancouver. Some work was undertaken by them at St. John's Victoria, but it seems to have soon languished. The first reference to East Indian missionary work in the diocese of New Westminster occurs in Bishop de Pencier's charge to synod in February,

1911,[24] when he reported that he had received an offer to come and labour among the East Indians from "a well-recommended Hindoo, in priest's orders in the Anglican Church in India." The committee on the Bishop's charge recommended that the Executive Committee should be asked, if possible, to provide funds for this purpose. However, the "well-recommended Hindoo, in priest's orders," never materialized but the Bishop did report to the following meeting of synod that "a good start has been made to reach some of the two thousand East Indians in the city of Vancouver." The mission was set up in All Saints' parish. An East Indian Mission Committee was formed with the Reverend H. C. Lewis Hooper, Rector of All Saints', as chairman. Cornelius E. Porter, a former Church Army captain, was appointed as catechist.

A further report was presented in 1913 by Porter himself which, although lengthy, does not do justice to the nature of the work being done. It reveals little of the state of the mission beyond the fact that it was addressed to Mohammedans, Hindus, and Sikhs, and apparently followed the usual pattern of first teaching them English as a preliminary to presenting the claims and promises of the Gospel. A year later Porter was dead, and the rector of All Saints' spoke most appreciatively of his work and influence. "Mr. Porter's wonderful knowledge of the Oriental character," he wrote, "and his command of, at least, three of the East Indian languages, stood him in good stead in his work. For a self-taught man he was one of the first East Indian linguists in Canada. He was a man 'full of the Holy Ghost and of faith,' and his zeal, in spite of the infirmities of advancing years, had a wonderful effect upon the native mind. His influence affected many classes apart from his Mission, and he was well known in Vancouver as a street preacher of force, and a quiet worker among certain men and women whom the Church does not usually reach."[25] With the death of the catechist and the imminence of the Great War, no one could be found to take his place; and the work of the East Indian Mission was discontinued, never to be resumed.

To return to the Provincial Board of Oriental Missions; at its formation financial aid was sought and received from the British Columbia and Yukon Church Aid Society, the Missionary Society of the Church in Canada, and the Woman's Auxiliary. By the end of 1919 there were a priest, the Reverend N. L. Ward, and a deacon, the Reverend George Lim Yuen, attached to the Chinese Mission, with catechists and lady missionaries in Vancouver and Victoria. Provision had been made for work in the diocese of Kootenay but nothing had actually been done. A worker was appointed at Vernon in the late 1920's.

The Japanese mission had a priest, the Reverend F. W. Cassilis Kennedy, as superintendent, while the assistant, the Reverend Bernard F. Oana, was abroad gaining practical experience in the Diocese of Osaka.[26] There were also catechists in Vancouver and in Prince Rupert, where a building had been erected with funds from the Anglican Forward Movement, the W.A., and the Japanese themselves. In addition to these workers there were lay missionaries and teachers in Vancouver. As a result of the combined efforts of these workers there was a steady stream of baptisms and confirmations in both Chinese and Japanese missions.

---

1 F. W. Howay & E. O. S. Scholefield, *British Columbia*, S. J. Clarke Publishing Co., Vancouver, 1914, Vol. II, p.567.
2 R. C. Lundin Brown, *British Columbia*, Royal Engineers' Press, New Westminster, 1863, p.52.
3 *Columbia Mission: Occasional Paper*, June, 1860, p.14.
4 *Columbia Mission Report*, 1862, p.48.
5 *Columbia Mission Report*, 1866, p.46.
6 *Columbia Mission Report*, 1868, p.37.

7 *Churchman's Gazette*, Vol. 12, No. 3, July, 1892.

8 *Churchman's Gazette*, Vol. 13, No. 3, July, 1893.

9 *Churchman's Gazette*, Vol. 13, No. 6, October, 1893.

10 Minutes of the Executive Committee, Synod of the Diocese of New Westminster, May 16th, 1900.

11 *Ibid.*

12 Proceedings, Synod of the Diocese of New Westminster, October, 1904, p.37.

13 F. W. Howay & E. O. S. Scholefield, *British Columbia*, Vol. II, p.577.

14 Proceedings, Synod of the Diocese of New Westminster, 1900, p.16.

15 *Ibid.*

16 Minutes of the Executive Committee, Synod of the Diocese of New Westminster, May 18th, 1904.

17 Proceedings, Synod of the Diocese of New Westminster, 1904, p.50.

18 Proceedings, Synod of the Diocese of New Westminster, June, 1912, p.66.

19 Has been spelled "Fiennes-Clinton" in earlier sources.

20 Proceedings, Synod of the Diocese of New Westminster, February, 1911, p. 40.

21 Proceedings, Synod of the Diocese of New Westminster, June, 1915, p.22.

22 Proceedings, Provincial Synod of British Columbia, May, 1917, pp.31, 32, & 50-2.

23 F. W. Howay, *British Columbia: The Making of a Province*, Ryerson, Toronto, 1928, p.266.

24 Proceedings, Synod of the Diocese of New Westminster, February, 1911, p.32.

25 Proceedings, Synod of the Diocese of New Westminster, June, 1914, p.90.

26 *Anglican Japanese Missions in Canada: An Historical Survey*, unpublished essay by the Reverend Timothy M. Nakayama, B.A., Anglican Theological College, Vancouver, 1956, p.10.

# 13

# The Anglican
# Theological
# College

ONE of the earliest suggestions for a missionary or theological college in what is now British Columbia came from the Reverend Charles Grenfell Nicolay who served for a time as Chaplain of King's College Hospital, London, and later went to Australia. In 1853 he embodied his proposal in a letter to William Ewart Gladstone. This began with a criticism of the Hudson's Bay Company, claiming that they cared only for profits and not for the natives. He had to admit, however, that no other body, and certainly not the Church of England, had been able to achieve much success in missionary ventures among the Indians. The solution, he felt, was a self-sustaining religious community which would include a principal or superior, and five fellows or brethren, preferably married men with families. "Of these two should be priests, to secure a continuance of sacramental administration; two might be medical men, who might also be in deacon's orders, . . . the two other might be laymen, . . . one, at least, should be, in the first instance, a sailor."[1]

Such an institution, he believed, would not only be self-supporting, a pleasant change from any previous missionary ventures, but would extend its influence throughout the region and ultimately "what was at first a Missionary College, must become at last the Colonial University."[2] Nicolay's vision was both farseeing and prophetic, and has found expression in many ways, not only in the provincial Theological College, but in such ventures as the Columbia Coast Mission.

When Bishop Hills first came to Victoria he expressed the conviction that "a college for training up young men in the colony for the several parts of the missionary work is urgently needed, together with industrial and other schools."[3]

As we have seen already some church schools were set up but nothing was done about a theological college for more than a generation. At the beginning of the present century there was again talk of a theological college, but this time it started in Vancouver, prompted, no doubt, by the opening of the McGill University College of British Columbia, forerunner of the present provincial university.

At first nothing more than a diocesan institution was contemplated and the moving spirit in its establishment was the Venerable E. W. S. Pentreath, B.D., Archdeacon of Columbia, although the Bishop of New Westminster, the Right Reverend J. C. Dart, was no less enthusiastic and told his diocesan synod in 1907 that there was urgent need of such a college.[4] About the same time it was announced that a gift of £200 had been received from the widow of the Reverend Edward Tritton Gurney, a graduate of Trinity College, Toronto, for the purchase of a building site, and a further £300 from the New England Company for the same purpose. In addition, £800 had been allocated by the New Westminster and Kootenay Missionary Association, an English auxiliary, for the college. This association later became the British Columbia and Yukon Church Aid Society and has been of great help to the church here.

A site for the proposed college was selected in the vicinity of Holy Trinity Church[5] but so rapid was the rise in the price of real estate that the transaction was not completed.[6] Shortly afterwards, however, Archdeacon Pentreath was able to report that land had been secured in the same vicinity near "where McGill is providing temporary lectures in science and arts."[7] Nothing more was done but early in 1908 the hope was expressed that work would begin on the college in the following autumn. Shortly afterwards Archdeacon Pentreath informed synod that a meeting of representative clergy in Vancouver had approved a constitution for the proposed college,[8] and that from a list of names submitted to her, Mrs. Tritton Gurney had selected that of St. Mark for its dedication. In the light of subsequent events one imagines that the continued delays were due in part to uncertainty regarding the location of the university, but also to a lack of interest if not to actual opposition by those who disagreed with the views of the sponsors.

The supporters of the college, probably with a view to strengthening their position and also because it seemed the logical thing to do, now sought the interest of other dioceses in British Columbia thus making the proposed college a provincial institution instead of merely a diocesan one. The year 1909 was the jubilee of the consecration of the first bishop of British Columbia and as part of the celebration the four dioceses of the province published a brochure called *Across the Plains to Sunset Land,* in which the proposed college figured prominently and was the object of an appeal for £30,000 for buildings, library, chapel and some endowments for the salaries of professors. Plans of the intended building were shown and there seemed every chance that it would soon become an accomplished fact. But there were still delays and in February 1910 Bishop Dart told his synod[9] that the site of the proposed University of British Columbia was still undecided and as it was hoped to have St. Mark's College close to it, building operations had been delayed.

It was at this point that some of the difficulties which seem to have contributed to the delay became apparent. The Reverend C. C. Owen, B.A., who had become Rector of Christ Church, Vancouver, in 1903, was a dominating personality of strong Evangelical convictions, beloved by all who shared his views, admired and revered by those who differed from him. Shortly after his arrival he found himself among a group of men who thought as he did, and who believed that they could have no part in the proposed provincial theological college. In December, 1908, a small group of these men met to discuss the situation. Probably the occasion of the meeting was suggested by the fact that Bishop Stringer, also a strong Evangelical, was passing through the city. At this meeting it was decided that a larger western conference of Evangelicals be held in the near future.

This larger conference took place in Vancouver on February 11th, 1909, "attended by five clergymen and five laymen, representing among them the three Dioceses of Columbia, New Westminster, and Yukon, and at which were received communications from Bishop Stringer of the Yukon and several laymen unable to attend strongly endorsing the movement. . . ."[10] It was then decided "to form a Pacific Coast Theological College on Evangelical English Church lines . . . to be known as Bishop Latimer College . . . conducted [on the lines] of Wycliffe College, Toronto."[11] The suggestion for the name of the new College seems to have come from Owen who pointed out that there was already a Ridley Hall at Cambridge, and colleges commemorating Wycliffe at Oxford and Toronto, but none in honour of Latimer.

It was hoped that the new college would begin its work in the following October "with a staff of two lecturers, one of whom might give part of his time to parochial work."[12] Following this meeting the Reverend A. E. O'Meara was sent to eastern Canada and to England to gain encouragement and financial support for the new venture.

O'Meara had been a lawyer who, after ordination, went to Tagish Lake, near Carcross. While there he became interested in the Indians and after leaving the Yukon became a self-appointed Indian advocate. While in England he approached the Church Missionary Society and the Colonial and Continental Church Society for aid. The latter society promised £200 per annum towards the stipend of the principal provided that they had a voice in his selection.

Writing to Owen to report this arrangement, O'Meara expressed the view that it would be "desirable to defer any announcement until after an actual decision to establish the College had been reached. "I think," he continued, "we agreed that our first step would then be to explain our plans to Bishop Perrin. You and I might together perform that interesting duty."[13] The Right Reverend W. W. Perrin was the Bishop of British Columbia and the senior bishop of the province, and O'Meara's gentle irony may be taken as an indication of the reception anticipated from official sources.

On May 26th, 1909, after O'Meara's return a further meeting was held at Christ Church, Vancouver, and the decision made to proceed with the establishment of Latimer Hall. A day or so before the meeting Owen called on Bishop Dart to acquaint him with the plans of the Evangelicals but he was not at home. In consequence, the first intimation the Bishop had of the intended college was from the newspaper report which appeared in the *Vancouver Province* on the day following the meeting. The

Bishop then wrote to Owen complaining that although he had been frequently to Christ Church no word of the proposal had ever reached him, and concluded, "of course, I could not recognize in any way your proposed rival Theological College in my diocese."[14]

He further emphasised his disapproval in his charge to the Synod of the Diocese of Kootenay a few days later by saying, "You all know that I have had in my mind for years the need of a theological college in this province, that steps have been taken to secure a site for it near the proposed university. . . . You may not know that towards the end of last month a meeting was held in Vancouver to discuss ways and means for building there an evangelical college, ostensibly for the purpose of training ministers for the Church of England. This movement I utterly condemn, and my brother bishop of Columbia entirely agrees with me."[15] Owen evidently wrote to the Bishop on July 19th, putting the case for Latimer with the assurance that he and his colleagues had "no disloyal feelings towards the Church authorities."[16]

To this letter Bishop Dart replied on July 22nd repeating his view that there was no place for a second college in Vancouver, and expressing his hope that the supporters of the proposed college would give up their opposition scheme and join heartily with the diocesan authorities in the establishment of St. Mark's College.

The supporters of Latimer still felt it necessary to pursue their intentions and a little later a committee consisting of the Reverend T. R. O'Meara, Principal of Wycliffe College; the Reverend Dr. H. J. Cody, of St. Paul's Church, Toronto; and Dr. Hoyles, President of Wycliffe College; along with Owen who was in the east at the time, was asked to suggest a suitable person for the principalship. Their choice fell upon the Reverend W. H.

Vance, M.A., a recent graduate of Wycliffe College, who was, at the time, Rector of the Church of the Ascension, Toronto. On June 29th, Owen wired to the Reverend A. H. Sovereign in Vancouver, "VANCE UNANIMOUS CHOICE: YOU TEACH DOGMATICS."[17] Thus the two lecturers had been found, for Sovereign could continue in his post as assistant curate at Christ Church and devote some of his time to the College. The Council of Bishop Latimer College received the recommendation but knowing that the C. & C.C.S. wished to have a voice in the appointment, decided that Vance should be offered the position of Lecturer and Organizing Secretary. Vance may have been aware of the situation but replied that he would consider nothing less than the principalship. This decision was conveyed to the Society in England and they agreed to his appointment. This much having been settled, Sovereign, as Secretary of the Council of the proposed College, wrote to Vance explaining the situation and offering him the principalship, which he ultimately accepted.

Vance moved to Vancouver in June, 1910 but the situation was complicated by the fact that Bishop Dart had died in April, and his successor, Bishop de Pencier, was not consecrated until July. The new Bishop was not convinced of the wisdom of the new venture and was not willing at that time to license Vance as Principal. For that reason in the Synod Journal of 1911 he was described as "Assistant Curate, Christ Church." During the summer a house at 1548 Haro Street was bought to accommodate the new College. The official opening took place on Friday, October 7th, 1910, and lectures began on the following Tuesday with the Reverend A. H. Sovereign, M.A., and the Reverend G. H. Wilson, B.A., assisting with the teaching until permanent professors were appointed. Shortly afterwards the Reverend H. R. Trumpour, M.A., B.D., and the Reverend H. G. Miller, M.A., retired principal of Huron College, were appointed to the staff as lecturers in New Testament Studies and Theology respectively.

The formation of Bishop Latimer College, while it did not take the church authorities altogether by surprise, certainly did not receive their commendation; and not unnaturally they were reluctant to award it any official recognition. In fact, the Bishops of British Columbia and New Westminster wrote to the C. & C.C.S. just before its opening "strongly deprecating the action of the committee in supporting Bishop Latimer College."[18]

For the next year or so Vance, walking warily and slowly, gained the approval of Bishop de Pencier. Writing to Mullins, of the C. & C.C.S. early in 1911 he remarked that "St. Mark's is further away than ever,"[19] while later in the year he reported that the Reverend J. Cooper Robinson, a Canadian missionary to Japan, had announced that he would send some men to be trained at Latimer. This, remarked Vance, would be a help.[20] As the year wore on there were further signs of progress—seven new applications and the prospect of a very considerable number of students for the next term; and then a very real triumph—official recognition by Bishop de Pencier. "The Bishop of New Westminster has accepted the position of 'visitor' to Latimer. . . ." wrote Vance.[21]

By this time he felt that Latimer was firmly established and that nothing could now disturb them. In any case, he remarked, nothing was heard of St. Mark's, and the general impression was that the matter had been abandoned for the time at least. Nothing, however, adds to the prestige of a college like graduates and as they would have none of their own in 1913, Vance wondered if the C. & C.C.S. would transfer one of their senior men from Wycliffe! It is hardly necessary to add that Mullins did not take very kindly to this amazing suggestion and the idea was dropped. By the third year of its existence Latimer had sixteen men, and a thirty-foot annex was added to the house on Haro Street to provide additional accommodation. The final location of the College was dependent upon the site chosen for the university but concerning this no decision was forthcoming. A year or so later Vance acquired control of the Chesterfield Boys' School in North Vancouver. He was careful to emphasise the fact that this was a purely personal venture and in no way connected with the College, but added that "it seemed wise to get a possible feeder to Latimer of this kind. It would have been used otherwise. . . ."[22]

While Latimer was developing in this way it was realised that two competing theological colleges—and the authorities had no intention of sacrificing St. Mark's—would not be in the best interests of the Church. In consequence, a memorandum was drawn up by the bishops of the province in connection with the British Columbia Jubilee Fund and called "The Plan for Theological Education in the Church of England in the Province of British Columbia," known afterwards more briefly as "The Plan." The plan provided for the establishment of an Anglican Theological College of British Columbia with which the two Halls, Latimer and St. Mark's, should be affiliated. The College which was incorporated by Act of the Provincial Legislature, 1915, amended 1921, was to have a Board of Governors made up of the bishops of the province, with clerical and lay representatives from each diocese. The Board would be responsible for the erection and maintenance of lecture rooms and library, the appointment and support of professors in subjects to be taken in common by all students, *e.g.* Old Testament studies and Apologetics, and the issuing of all diplomas. Each of the Halls was to be governed by an independent council which would erect and maintain its residences and chapel, collect its own funds in addition to those allocated by the Board of Governors, and employ its own teaching staff.

Meanwhile, the sponsors of St. Mark's Hall had not abandoned their plans and advantage was taken of the consecration of the Right Reverend J. C. Roper, on St. Matthias' Day, 1912, to hold a meeting in Victoria on the evening before. The clergy present concluded that the time was ripe for the formation of a college and decided to present their views to the bishops following the consecration service. This was done and plans were made for a meeting at St. Paul's, Vancouver, on St. Mark's Day, when the organization could be completed. At that meeting a constitution was adopted, the corporation elected, and a committee appointed to proceed with the planning of the Hall. Shortly afterwards property was obtained at 1249 Davie Street, and the Reverend C. A. Seager, M.A., Rector of Vernon, appointed Principal. The College began its work on October 1st, 1912 with nine students, eight of whom lived in the residence.

The Principal, in the first issue of the *St. Mark's Hall Bulletin*,[23] assured his readers that the College was not to be an extreme High Church institution and that "it was not designed to turn out men of a certain 'stripe,' but men who, sound in knowledge and with a basis of broad but definite Churchmanship, should learn to think for themselves."[24]

The two Halls were duly incorporated by acts of the Provincial Legislature, Latimer in 1911, and St. Mark's in 1913.

For the next few years the Halls continued their separate existence each with a few students, each struggling to make ends meet financially, each gravely hampered by the Great War of 1914-1918. The formation of the Anglican Theological College marked the first official link between them and during the session 1914-1915 two sets of common lectures were given, one on "Missions in Japan," by the Reverend C. H. Shortt, M.A., and the other in Sociology by the Reverend Robert Connell. At the annual meeting of the Board of Governors in 1915 it was decided that a "common" Old Testament Professor should be appointed, but owing to the exigencies of war no appointment was made and the work continued to be done by the faculties of the two Halls. In the next year G. H. Cowan, a member of the Latimer Hall Council, wrote to Bishop Du Vernet urging the greater unification of the two institutions.[26] The Bishop, who was a keen supporter of Latimer Hall and also President of the Anglican Theological College, replied saying that he felt that nine-tenths of the course should be in common and that Ecclesiology (doctrine of the Church) was the main subject which needed to be taught separately. Were this done each Hall would need only a Principal.[27]

In 1918, Dr. Seager, Principal of St. Mark's Hall, moved to Toronto where he first became Rector of St. Matthew's and later Provost of Trinity College. In the words of Bishop Roper he had made an excellent beginning "and it was financial pressure only, that made him give up. All . . . were loath to let him go."[28] His successor was the Reverend C. H. Shortt, then a missionary in Japan who returned to Canada to take up the appointment. Shortt was an eirenic soul, completely devoid of personal ambition, concerned only for the well being of the Church and College, and with a deep personal interest in his students. When the amalgamation of the two Halls was finally consummated Bishop Schofield wrote to him, "May I seize this opportunity of expressing to you my warm appreciation of the part you have yourself played in bringing about this so promising situation: under God, we owe more than most people are aware to you. . . ."[29]

With the end of the war it became apparent that difficulties of men and money would not be decreased while the two Halls continued to function separately. A new temper was abroad which had little time for denominational differences and less for theological controversies within a single communion. At the first meeting of the Provincial Synod after the war, at St. Paul's, Vancouver, in January of 1920, the matter of the two Halls was discussed and the feeling expressed that they should be more closely integrated. A resolution to that effect was adopted unanimously.

A committee on closer co-operation was set up which met that same month and agreed on some preliminary steps. It received a resolution from the combined student body of the two Halls affirming "that it is their unanimous opinion that there should be one united student body living in one hostel."[30] There being a general realisation that the amalgamation of the two Halls was both desirable and inevitable the committee suggested steps by which it could be carried out. Recommendations were made on the necessary changes in the constitution. It was agreed that the Reverend W. H. Vance should be Principal of the College, and the Reverend C. H. Shortt, Vice-Principal, with the title of Warden. An interim policy for the best use of the buildings belonging to the two Halls was also discussed. A further meeting of the committee was held in Victoria a few days later when some of the practical details were discussed and decisions made.

On May 5th, 1920 the conclusion of the committee "that the present plan which contemplates a central college with two residential halls should be revised to provide for a college with residence for all the students in attendance"[31] was presented in the name of the Provincial Synod to the Board of Governors of the Anglican Theological College, which moved at once to put it into effect.

The St. Mark's property was sold but the chapel moved to Haro Street, since Latimer Hall, with its annex, was the larger of the two. In 1922, the house next door, 1542 Haro Street, was purchased for additional accommodation.[32] Shortly after the decision to amalgamate, Vance wrote to the Secretary of the C. & C.C.S., concerning the arrangement of the chapel, "I have agreed to place the cross on the table. The lights are to be done away with; also wafer bread. They had both of these. The Eastward position is to be optional. Vestments are not allowed. This will give a general idea of the spirit of the new plan."[33]

As we have suggested earlier, the spirit of Christian unity was in the air, and at times it almost seemed to be a demand for re-union at any price. It is not surprising therefore that in 1922 Dr. S. D. Scott, Chairman of the Board of Ryerson (Methodist) College suggested to the authorities of Westminster (Presbyterian) Hall and the Anglican Theological College that enquiries be made into the possibilities of co-operation across denominational lines in theological education. A meeting was held in Wesley Church, Vancouver, on April 22nd, 1922, attended by representatives of the three Colleges, at which it was agreed to suggest to the respective Boards that a plan of co-operation similar to that in effect in Montreal should be adopted. The Board of the Anglican Theological College, after investigation of such schemes elsewhere, decided to engage in the venture with certain reservations, Bishop Doull of Kootenay dissenting.

A joint committee met a few weeks later and divided the curriculum into "Reserved" and "Common" subjects. Bishop Doull continued to express his opposition, asserting that such co-operation was a breach of faith with those who had founded St. Mark's Hall, which, if persisted in, would leave him no alternative but to sever his connection with the College. Vance, in discussing the matter by letter with Archbishop Du Vernet, seemed far less concerned with the effect of Bishop Doull's withdrawal than with the hypothetical question of his legal ability to withdraw from the College. At the same time the Diocese of Calgary withdrew its support although with less justification since their action was taken purely on the grounds of an inaccurate report in the *Canadian Churchman*.[34]

The fear in the minds of both bishops seemed to run along the same lines and was caused, first of all, by the fact that tensions in Anglicanism were still very recent and painful, and great damage might be done within and without if the Church through co-operation with other religious bodies, appeared uncertain of her own distinctive position. Then, too, the Methodists and Presbyterians seemed to be rushing into a union for which they were ill-prepared and which showed every sign of issuing in ill-will and litigation.

The objections from Calgary came to an end with the retirement in 1926 of Bishop Pinkham. Personal relations between Vance and Bishop Doull continued to be very cordial during the period of official estrangement and ultimately Doull returned to his place in the councils of the College. His return, as he himself said, was influenced by three factors; first, that no sacrifice of principle had been involved in the co-operative scheme; second, that the scheme of union which brought into being the United Church of Canada had been carried through without in any way endangering the Anglican position; third, and most significant of all, that with the election of the Right Reverend Walter R. Adams as Bishop of Cariboo he had gained an ally of like mind who would stand with him in the cause of orthodoxy. The scheme of co-operation was reviewed and extended in 1925, and again in 1926. In 1929 grave doubt concerning the situation was expressed by the Bishops of Kootenay and Cariboo but the general impression seemed to be that since the plan had been carried on for almost eight years with results which were apparently wholly beneficial there was no reason to discontinue the system of co-operation.

There remains to be discussed the twofold problem of buildings and university affiliation. It will be remembered that from the beginning concern had been expressed by almost everyone connected with theological education that the College, or Colleges, should work as closely as possible with the University; and this meant having the buildings as close to it as possible. The failure of the University authorities to decide on a site had been one of the major reasons for the delay in the opening of St. Mark's Hall. The decision concerning the University came in 1920 when the Minister of Education announced that Point Grey had been selected and that the work on the buildings there would begin in the following year. In such circumstances, said Dr. Vance in his report to the Board of Governors,[35] the College should be prepared to move to the permanent site at the same time. Negotiations with the University began, and there was also some discussion of the possible advantages of a larger site just outside the University grounds, but for a year or two nothing was done. Work on the Science Building (the present Chemistry Building) which had begun in 1914 but had been delayed by the war, was resumed in 1923, and the University commenced lectures in its new quarters in the fall of 1925.

Writing to Archbishop Du Vernet, the Principal said concerning the annual meeting of the Board of Governors, ". . . the big question will be the decision about buildings at Point Grey. With the air filled with the idea of university buildings it would be so much easier to get money now than at any other time. I feel that so far as the success of the undertaking is concerned it is now or not for years. . . ."[36]

Unfortunately the minutes of the 1924 annual meetings have disappeared but evidently the idea of building at Point Grey on land leased from the University was endorsed, and during the summer Vance wrote to the Archbishop asking him to write a short commendation for the brochure which was to launch the appeal for $125,000, the amount required for the construction of the first unit of the new College building. This was almost

Archbishop Du Vernet's last official act as President of the College for, on October 22nd, 1924, he died after a period of failing health.

The appeal was launched and Vance threw himself wholeheartedly into the business of raising the funds needed for the project. The turning of the first sod was performed by the Governor-General, Lord Willingdon, on April 13, 1927 and the College was officially opened by the Primate, the Most Reverend S. P. Matheson, on Wednesday, November 9th, 1927.

A vital part of the connection with the University was not only physical proximity but actual affiliation and a voice in the affairs of the institution. Application for affiliation was made and granted in 1922. Affiliation brings to the College both tangible and intangible benefits and also enables the theological colleges generally to make their contribution to the life of the University The tangible benefits are representation on the University Senate through which the College has a voice in academic affairs; and the provision for "Religious Knowledge Options" through which any registered student of the College may present certain theological courses for credit in the Arts course. The intangible benefits are obviously more difficult to define. They would include a little of the reflected glory of the University—obviously the academic reputation of a smaller institution is to some extent overshadowed by its larger neighbour and for the College this has been, on the whole, beneficial. There is also the contact between minds both at the faculty and student levels, together with opportunities for members of the College to enjoy the facilities of the University. In this latter one of the most significant benefits is the use of the University Library.

On the other side the presence of the College makes its own contribution, standing for a measure of Christian conviction in a society where agnosticism and secularism are sometimes apparent.

The faculty and students of the College have always mixed with those of other faculties and have, thereby, been called upon to defend their faith and bear a Christian witness.

1 *A proposal to establish a Missionary College on the North West coast of British America, in a letter to the Right Honourable William Ewart Gladstone, M.P., from the Reverend Charles Grenfell Nicolay, F.R.G.S., Librarian of King's College, London,* Saunders and Stanford, London, 1853.
2 *Ibid.*
3 *Columbia Mission: Occasional Paper,* 1860, p.34.
4 Proceedings, Synod of the Diocese of New Westminster, 1907, p.27.
5 *Work for the Far West,* No. XXXIV, October, 1905, p.12.
6 *Work for the Far West,* No. XXXVII, July, 1906, p.16.
7 *Work for the Far West,* No. XXXVIII, October, 1906, p.19.
8 Proceedings, Synod of the Diocese of New Westminster, 1908, p.28.
9 Proceedings, Synod of the Diocese of New Westminster, February, 1910, p.25.
10 Records of The Anglican Theological College of B. C.
11 College Records.
12 College Records.
13 A. E. O'Meara to C. C. Owen, April 20th, 1909, College Records.
14 There are some difficulties about this letter. The only known extant copy is in a printed circular in the College files where it is dated July 19th, 1909. As it was quoted by the Bishop in his charge to the Kootenay Synod on June 9th, 1909, it must actually have been written in the early days of June.
15 Proceedings of the Synod of the Diocese of Kootenay, June 9th and 10th, 1909, pp.14-15.
16 Quoted by the Bishop in his reply. The original is not extant. The Bishop's reply is contained in a printed circular in the College files.
17 College Records.
18 Letter, J. D. Mullins to C. C. Owen, February 5th, 1909, College Records.
19 Letter, W. H. Vance to J. D. Mullins, February 14th, 1911, College Records.
20 Letter, W. H. Vance to J. D. Mullins, May 22nd, 1911, College Records.
21 Letter, W. H. Vance to J. D. Mullins, December 9th, 1911, College Records.

22 Letter, W. H. Vance to J. D. Mullins, September 12th, 1913, College Records.

23 *St. Mark's Hall Bulletin*, Vol. 1, No. 1., November, 1912, College Records.

24 *Ibid.*

25 *Ibid.*

26 Letter, G. H. C. [Cowan] to Archbishop Du Vernet, August 10th, 1916, College Records.

27 Letter, Archbishop Du Vernet to G. H. Cowan, August 17th, 1916, College Records.

28 Letter, Rt. Rev. J. C. Roper to C. H. Shortt, May 13th, 1918, College Records.

29 Letter, Rt. Rev. C. D. Schofield to C. H. Shortt, February 25th, 1929, College Records.

30 Resolution from the student body in the College Records.

31 Statement by the Archbishop of Caledonia, College Records.

32 Minutes of the Board of Governors, Anglican Theological College, May 3rd, 1922.

33 Letter, W. H. Vance to J. D. Mullins, May 15th, 1920, College Records.

34 Letter, Bishop of Calgary to W. H. Vance, July 2, 1933, Anglican Theological College, Vancouver.

35 Report, May 5th, 1929, College Records.

36 Letter, W. H. Vance to Archbishop Du Vernet, April 9th, 1924, College Records.

# 14

# Further Steps
# In Organization

THE building of railways in British Columbia has had, as elsewhere, a very great effect upon immigration and settlement, and consequently, upon the expansion of church work. There was first the Canadian Pacific Railway line which reached Port Moody in 1885 and was extended to Vancouver two years later. This was followed by the Crow's Nest Railway to Kootenay Lake, completed in 1900; the Canadian Northern which reached Vancouver by way of the Yellowhead Pass in 1914; and the Grand Trunk Pacific Railway which went by the same pass to Prince Rupert and was opened in 1915. In the southern part of the province the Kootenay Central Railway linking Golden and Fort Steele was opened in 1911 while the Kettle Valley Railway was completed and in operation shortly after.

As a result of these developments two new dioceses have been established in the province in the twentieth century, and all six dioceses welded into an ecclesiastical province with its own metropolitan. First came the Diocese of Kootenay. As a matter of fact, Kootenay may claim to antedate the century by a few months if not more. The population in the Kootenays had already grown tremendously through the influx of miners before the opening of the Crow's Nest Railway, and there was talk of divid- ing the diocese of New Westminster which comprised the whole of the lower mainland. A memorial signed by more than 130 clergy and laity of the Kootenay district was received by the New Westminster Diocesan Synod in 1899 and the division of the diocese was approved in principle.[1] Committees were appointed in Nelson and Vancouver to draw up recommendations concern- ing procedure. The Bishop, in commending the necessity for the change to supporters in England pointed out that it would be a great saving in expense since it was "better for one man [the Bishop] to go up than for fifty or sixty people to come down."[2] Then, he added, there were local needs in Kootenay which could only be adequately met by a local synod.

The committees met many times and at the Synod of New Westminster in November, 1899, it was recommended that the division of the diocese should take place immediately with the 120th meridian as the boundary line between the older diocese and the new one.[3] The Bishop of New Westminster and his successors were to have episcopal charge of the new diocese until its bishopric endowment fund reached the sum of $40,000. If the fund was completed during the episcopate of Bishop Dart he was to have the option of becoming Bishop of Kootenay or retaining the See of New Westminster. Otherwise, the Kootenay Diocesan Synod would proceed to elect its own bishop. Provision was also made for the assistance of the Archdeacon of Columbia to continue until an archdeacon in the new diocese could be appointed. Mission grants and funds then being used in the Kootenay district were to continue and to be administered in future by the Executive Committee of the new Synod. Church property was to be similarly transferred to the Synod of Kootenay. Provincial legislation was to be sought to confirm the change as soon as possible, and the Archbishop of Canterbury asked to give his assent to the establishment of the new diocese. The resolution was presented to the synod by the Hon. T. Mayne Daly, Q.C., and A. E. Crease, both of Nelson, and passed unanimously.

News of the decision was telegraphed to the Most Reverend Robert Machray, Archbishop of Rupert's Land and Primate of All Canada, who replied extending his congratulations on the important step which had been taken. Later, the new synod expressed the wish that the new bishop, when elected, should be consecrated by the Primate of All Canada thus helping to emphasise the growing unity of the Canadian Church.[4]

The first meeting of the new Kootenay synod took place at Nelson on May 30th and 31st, 1900, with fifteen of the eighteen clergy, and twenty-eight lay delegates present. Nelson was designated as the see city with St. Saviour's as the pro-cathedral church. Immediate steps were to be taken for the building up of the episcopal endowment fund but this was hindered by the fact that the bishopric endowment of the mother diocese was still inadequate. Provision was also to be made for the erection of a see house in Nelson. In all, the first synod was, as Archdeacon Pentreath said, "most harmonious and at times enthusiastic."[5] Returning to Vancouver the Archdeacon reported to the New Westminster Executive Committee that the synod had been held and had asked "that it [the Committee] would continue present financial arrangements as to the Kootenay Diocese and its share of the general funds up to September 30th next, after which the new diocese would administer its own funds and control all its own business."[6]

By Easter, 1901, it was reported that there had been a general increase in the strength of the new diocese. There were now 1,005 communicants, a gain of 39; and during the year there had been 222 baptisms, an increase of 42. There were 556 Sunday School pupils, and 56 teachers, gains of 59 pupils and six teachers. All the parishes would shortly be filled, and new missions were contemplated at Moyie, Lardeau, and Arrowhead. In 1902, the Reverend F. H. Graham, B.A., came to Nelson as rector of the pro-cathedral, thus beginning a long connection with the diocese broken finally by his death in 1958.

Funds for the episcopal endowment did not accumulate as fast as had been hoped and in 1902 the Kootenay Synod recommended that "a Memorial be presented to the General Synod asking that Synod to make a grant of half the income of the bishop until the Endowment is completed, conditional on the balance being provided from other sources, . . ."[7] This, however, was not possible and instead the M.S.C.C. made a grant of $1,200 per annum, beginning in January, 1904, towards the stipend of a missionary archdeacon.[8] Shortly afterwards the Bishop announced that he had appointed the Reverend Henry Beer, Vicar of Kaslo, as Archdeacon of Kootenay. Archdeacon Beer came to Ontario in his youth and became a school teacher. After his ordination he served for some years in the Diocese of Algoma and subsequently in parishes in Minnesota. On the appointment of the Right Reverend Peter Trimble Rowe, a Canadian serving in the United States as Bishop of Alaska, Beer volunteered to accompany him and was given charge of the parish of Juneau. From there he went to Kaslo.

A decade after the foundation of the diocese numbers were still growing but the endowment fund had not reached the point where a bishop could be elected. By that time the amount required had risen to £10,000 of which £6,400 had been collected including three grants of £1,000 each from the S.P.G., the Colonial Bishoprics Fund, and the S.P.C.K. By 1913 Bishop de Pencier could write "the endowment fund for the new Bishopric of Kootenay is now completed, and it is hoped before the year is out a Bishop of Kootenay will be consecrated."[9] The electoral synod actually met on November 25th, 1914, when their choice fell upon the Very Reverend Alexander John Doull, M.A., Dean of British Columbia. Dean Doull was born in 1870 and was by upbringing a Presbyterian. After taking his degree at Oxford and a year at Cuddesdon he was ordained to a curacy at Leeds Parish Church which he left after three years to become assistant curate at the Church of the Advent, Montreal. He was later rector of the same church for nine years before moving to Victoria in 1910. Following his election he was consecrated in Christ Church Cathedral, Victoria, on St. Matthias' Day, 1915, and took up residence in Vernon.

The first suggestion of a possible further division of the Diocese of New Westminster came from Bishop de Pencier who had succeeded Bishop Dart in 1910. In his charge to synod in 1912 he said, "I contemplate the formation of another Rural Deanery, comprising Ashcroft and Kamloops and the northern parishes, just as soon as the lines of railroad indicate the most effective way of grouping these scattered parishes."[10] Not long afterwards the clergy of the Rural Deanery of Lytton discussed the matter at a chapter meeting and suggested that not only should the Rural Deanery be divided but that a new diocese should be constituted.[11] The announcement of this decision was embodied in a report to synod presented by the Reverend H. S. Akehurst, Rector of Kamloops. Appended to the report was the motion that ". . . the Bishop be requested to take the necessary steps for the subdivision of the Diocese of New Westminster by cutting off some of that portion which is included in the Yale, Cariboo, and Similkameen districts and forming it into a new diocese."

The resolution, after some discussion, was carried unanimously and referred to a special committee on the division of the diocese.

When the committee met on the following day there was a lengthy discussion of the ways and means of carrying out the proposed partition. As the provision of an episcopal endowment was one of the most important factors it was decided to ask the Bishop to communicate with the British Columbia Church Aid Society, thanking them for their generous help in the past, and enquiring to what extent they would feel able to assist in this new development. The Society replied that $2,000 had already been set aside towards the endowment.[12] This done, it was then decided that the sanction of the Primate should be sought and that as a matter of courtesy the other bishops in the province should be informed of what had been done.

The congregation of St. Paul's, Kamloops, were keenly interested in the new diocese believing that the appointment of a missionary bishop for the Cariboo would be of great benefit to the whole Church. At a meeting held in June, 1913, the congregation suggested Kamloops as the most suitable centre for the see city and undertook, were it selected, "to provide a site suitable for a Cathedral Church and an Episcopal residence, to do their share, when called upon, in the erection of such buildings, and in the meantime to supply their due proportion of any reasonable amount needed for the rent of a temporary residence for the Bishop. . . ."[13]

The resolution creating the new Diocese of Cariboo was passed by the executive committee of the New Westminster Synod on January 20th, 1914, when it declared "that a new diocese to be called the Diocese of Cariboo be, and hereby is, formed." Its boundaries were defined as follows: "from the point where the summit of the Cascade range touches the present northwestern boundary of the Diocese of New Westminster, along the summit of the Cascade mountains to the mouth of the Fraser canyon one mile north-east of Yale, thence east to the 120th meridian, and north to the former boundary of the Diocese of New Westminster, and along the line of boundary already defined as the southern boundary of the Diocese of Caledonia to the starting point." Steps were also taken to send the provincial government authorities a copy of the resolutions dealing with the partition and informing them that a meeting of the new synod would shortly be called.

Soon after these steps had been taken the Provincial Synod of British Columbia came into being and held its first meeting at Christ Church Cathedral, Victoria, in February, 1914. The Bishop of New Westminster reported the steps which had been taken regarding the formation of the Diocese of Cariboo to this meeting of the Provincial Synod, explaining that as there had been no provincial organization in existence when the undertaking was begun the precedent followed was that established in the setting apart of the Diocese of Kootenay. The Bishop of Caledonia who, as senior bishop, presided at the Synod, ruled that the steps already taken should be endorsed and that authority should be given to proceed along the lines indicated by the Bishop of New Westminster. This was done by unanimous vote. [14]

The final steps in formation of the new see were taken at the 32nd session of the New Westminster Diocesan Synod on June 11th, 1914, when a basis of division was adopted almost identical with the one relating to Kootenay fourteen years earlier. The Bishop of New Westminster and his successors were to retain episcopal oversight until the endowment fund of the new diocese was adequate to permit the election of a Bishop of Cariboo. Should this happen during Bishop de Pencier's episcopate he was to have the choice of remaining Bishop of New Westminster or going to Cariboo. Otherwise the new diocese would elect its own bishop. The Trust Funds belonging to New Westminster remained intact with that diocese but other funds and grants enjoyed by parishes and missions in the new diocese were transferred to the control of its executive committee. The Venerable E. W. W. Pugh, Archdeacon of Yale, the Reverend L. Dawson, Principal of St. George's Indian School, Lytton, and the Reverend H. S. Akehurst, Rector of Kamloops, were appointed as a committee to arrange for the necessary legislation.

The first session of the new synod was held at St. Alban's, Ashcroft, on October 28th, 1914 when the necessary work of organization was carried out. The Act of Incorporation was passed by the Provincial Legislature early in 1915, and a further meeting of the synod held on June 30th to ratify the constitution. Thus the fifth diocese in what had originally been the Diocese of British Columbia came into being. Once again, however, the problem remained of providing an adequate episcopal endowment and this time it was hampered by the Great War of 1914-1918 with the result that the fund was not completed until the early 1920's.

Finally, the Synod of Cariboo met on May 14th, 1925 and elected the Reverend Walter Robert Adams, M.A., (Dunelm.) as the first bishop. Adams had always been interested in the missionary work of the Church and used to tell how, when he was curate of Lambeth, he had attended a meeting at the offices of the S.P.G. Opening his eyes after a prayer he saw on the wall before him a map of western Canada with its vast open spaces which were rapidly filling up with settlers. That decided him, and for the next few years he laboured in prairie parishes afterwards serving as Assistant Secretary of the Archbishops' Western Canada Fund. He later became Chief Inspector of Church Schools in the Diocese of Southwark, which post he held at the time of his election to the see of Cariboo. He returned to Canada during the summer of 1925 and was consecrated by the Right Reverend A. U. de Pencier, then Acting Metropolitan of British Columbia, with the assistance of other nearby bishops, in St. Paul's Church, Kamloops on September 29th.

There remains to be discussed the formation of the Ecclesiastical Province of British Columbia, the constitution of its synod, and the appointment of the first metropolitan. Very early in the history of the Christian Church neighbouring dioceses formed themselves into provinces similar to the civil dioceses and provinces. Each ecclesiastical province had as its president a metropolitan, the bishop of the mother church in the province who, after the fourth century, was generally styled an archbishop. Within the province the archbishop enjoyed a primacy of honour and presided over the meetings of its synod. As the Church expanded in the modern era it was natural that its organization should have included the formation of provinces. The ecclesiastical province of Canada came into being in 1861, followed by that of Rupert's Land in 1875. In 1893, at the formation of the general synod, it was decided that metropolitans in Canada should follow the ancient usage and be given the title of archbishop.

At the first meeting of the Rupert's Land Provincial Synod the Metropolitan, Bishop Machray, was asked by his comprovincials to write to the Bishop of British Columbia, "inviting his diocese to take such action as may lead to its union with the Ecclesiastical Diocese [*sic*] of Rupert's Land."[15] The invitation was considered at the first meeting of the newly constituted British Columbia Diocesan Synod and the conclusion reached that although the invitation was appreciated action concerning it would be premature. In 1880, after the creation of the Dioceses of Caledonia and New Westminster, Bishop Hills spoke at some length in his charge to synod[16] of the possibility of establishing an ecclesiastical province in British Columbia. He cited many of the ancient authorities and gave examples of such provinces already existing. In addition, he said, a province was in course of formation in the West Indies and the Church in the United States had been considering the matter. The members of synod, having considered this recommendation, expressed the opinion that immediate steps should be taken to organize a provincial synod, and clerical and lay delegates were elected to represent the diocese. In spite of this nothing further was done although for some years thereafter representatives were elected at each synod to attend a conference for the formation of a Provincial Synod. In 1888 interest was revived slightly by the suggestion of a general synod, and the Bishop used the occasion to include another short lecture in his charge on the significance of provincial synods.

A few days after the April, 1888, session of the British Columbia Diocesan Synod the long delayed meetings of representatives from the Dioceses of British Columbia and New Westminster was held in Victoria.[17] The Bishop of British Columbia was elected to take the chair, and it was agreed that the purpose of the meeting was deliberative only. The practical results of a provincial synod were discussed and it was resolved that the three dioceses then existing in British Columbia should constitute the Province of Columbia. It was also recommended that the see of British Columbia should be the metropolitan see. At the close of the meeting a committee was appointed to draft a constitution and to arrange for future meetings. For the next few years, however, the matter of a provincial synod was overshadowed by plans for, and the actual formation of, the general synod in 1893, but in 1909 a conference of clergy and laity was held in Victoria to re-open the matter. Then, in the following year the New Westminster Diocesan Synod passed a resolution affirming its conviction that the time had arrived "when

*First meeting of the Provincial Synod of British Columbia, February 18-20, 1914.*

*The Anglican Theological College,*
*Haro Street, Vancouver, about 1922.*

*Anglican Theological College shortly*
*after its opening in 1927.*

it would be for the benefit of the Church that a Provincial Organization be formed for the Church of British Columbia."[18] No
action was directed to be taken but a further meeting of diocesan
representatives, this time from the four dioceses, was held at St.
Paul's, Vancouver, on July 26th, 1910, from which a resolution
was sent to the general synod recommending the formation of an
Ecclesiastical Province of British Columbia coterminous with the
boundaries of the civil province, and requesting confirmation of
the draft constitution which accompanied it.[19]

The request was granted and the senior bishop in British
Columbia was requested to summon the delegates from the
various dioceses. It was felt wise, however, to defer this until
the Bishop of Kootenay had been elected. When this election
did not take place as soon as had been expected the Provincial
Synod was summoned and met at Christ Church Cathedral,
Victoria, on Wednesday, February 18th, 1914. At this meeting, over which the Right Reverend F. H. Du Vernet presided,
as the senior bishop, he explained briefly the steps which had
led to the formation of the Synod after which a constitution was
drafted and adopted. Bishop Du Vernet was elected Metropolitan by the House of Bishops and thus became the Archbishop of
Caledonia and Metropolitan of British Columbia. In this way
the ecclesiastical organization of the province was complete. It
had begun with a single diocese with only one or two parishes,
but by 1914 there were four dioceses established with the
prospect of a fifth.

---

1 *Work for the Far West*, January, 1900, p.9.
2 *Ibid.*, p.6.
3 Proceedings, Synod of The Diocese of New Westminster, Nov.8,
   1899, quoted in a letter to the author from the Bishop of Kootenay,
   Oct. 10, 1958.
4 Robert Machray, *Life of Robert Machray*, Macmillan, Toronto:
   1909, p.440.

5 *Work for the Far West*, July, 1900, p.13.
6 Minutes of the Executive Committee of the Synod of the Diocese of New Westminster, July 11th, 1900.
7 *Work for the Far West*, October, 1902, No. XXII, p.16.
8 *Work for the Far West*, January, 1904, No. XXVII, p.17.
9 British Columbia Church Aid Society, *Year Book*, 1913, p.150.
10 Proceedings, Synod of the Diocese of New Westminster, June, 1912, p.40.
11 Proceedings, Synod of the Diocese of New Westminster, June, 1913, p.103.
12 Minutes of the Executive Committee of the Synod of the Diocese of New Westminster, August 3rd, 1913.
13 Minutes of the Executive Committee of the Synod of the Diocese of New Westminster, June, 1913.
14 Proceedings of the Synod of the Ecclesiastical Province of British Columbia, February, 1914, p.24.
15 Proceedings of the Synod of the Diocese of British Columbia, December, 1875, pp.34 and 38.
16 Proceedings, Synod of the Diocese of British Columbia, August, 1880, p.17.
17 Proceedings, Synod of the Diocese of British Columbia, June, 1888, p.29.
18 Proceedings, Synod of the Diocese of New Westminster, February, 1910, p.17.
19 Proceedings, Synod of the Diocese of New Westminster, February, 1911, p.20.

# 15

# Growth of the Church in the Far North

$I$T HAS been noted already that until the advent of railways the Rocky Mountains formed an almost impassable barrier between the Pacific slope and the rest of British North America. In consequence, British Columbia's connections were directly with Great Britain by sea, and to a lesser degree with Portland and San Francisco. A glance at the map will show, however, that for much of the far north the most direct line of communication lay along the rivers draining into the Arctic Ocean. Thus the earliest missionaries to the Mackenzie River and Yukon valleys came by this route from Winnipeg and Edmonton.

David Anderson became the first Bishop of Rupert's Land in 1849, and arrived to find himself confronted with a diocese so extensive that it was impossible to administer. Nevertheless, he gave himself wholeheartedly to the work and sought to build up a staff of fellow labourers. Among those who came to share in the undertaking was James Hunter who, after his training at the

Church Missionary College, Islington, served first at Lac La Ronge and then at Cumberland House.

In 1858 Archdeacon Hunter, as he had become, left his charge at Red River and set out in company with one of the Hudson's Bay Company's fur brigades to visit the northwest. The Roman Catholics had, as their custom was, sent missionaries through the area during the 1840's visiting Ile a la Crosse, Methy Portage, Lac la Biche, Edmonton, and Lac Ste. Anne, thus proving, to their own satisfaction at least, their inalienable and exclusive right to carry on missionary work in the areas visited. During the same period their work was strengthened considerably by the arrival of several Oblates of Mary Immaculate, a missionary order founded at Marseilles in 1815. Roman Catholic concern for their preserves was increased by the report of Hunter's proposed tour. "In 1858 an event which took everybody by surprise rendered the services of all newcomers into the vineyard of the Lord especially welcome. Suddenly it was learned that an archdeacon of the Church of England, the Reverend James Hunter, was going north, bent on proselytizing among the Indians in favour of his own sect, . . ."[1] So wrote the Oblate historian, Morice, and on the very brigade with which the archdeacon travelled there were five French Roman Catholic priests going to do what they could to offset the Anglican venture.[2]

Hunter pursued his way unshaken, and after a journey of nearly two thousand miles in a little over two months he reached Fort Simpson, the principal post in the Mackenzie River district. He spent the following winter in the north and visited Forts Liard, Norman, and Good Hope. During his stay he preached to the Slavi Indians and baptized nine of them. He also saw some of the Tudukh or Loucheux Indians and would dearly have loved to press on and visit them in the Yukon valley but that was impossible. In the following summer the archdeacon returned to the

Red River and the Reverend William West Kirkby (later Archdeacon) was sent to undertake work among both whites and
Indians with Fort Simpson as his headquarters. The jealous
Morice spoke of him as "a Red River schoolmaster, . . . who
was ordained for the occasion" but went on to admit that he
"proved to be a most active and resourceful man."[3] While at
Fort Simpson Kirkby built what he described as "a little gem of
a church"[4] and then in May, 1861, he set off for the Yukon.
Down the Mackenzie he went, accompanied by two Indian boys,
up the Peel River and over the summit of the Rocky Mountains
until he came to La Pierre's House where he found himself in
the midst of the Tudukh Indians. Not content to remain there
he pressed on until he came to Fort Yukon at the confluence
of the Yukon and Porcupine rivers, the furthest outpost of the
Hudson's Bay Company.

The news of Kirkby's journey so stirred the people of Red
River that a young "country-born" (that is, of mixed blood)
missionary, the Reverend Robert McDonald, offered to go to
the Tudukh Indians.[5] He had been at Fort Yukon less than two
years when his health seemed to fail, and he wrote to the Bishop
imploring him to send another missionary should he, McDonald,
not survive. The letter reached Bishop Anderson just as he
reached England to retire. He read it from the pulpit of St.
Bride's Church, London, at a C.M.S. Anniversary service in
May, 1865, and added, "Shall no one come forward to take
up the standard of the Lord as it drops from his hands . . . ?"[6]
Among those in the congregation was the Reverend William
Carpenter Bompas, a young Lincolnshire curate, and at the close
of the service he walked into the vestry and offered to undertake
the commission.

A week or so later he was ordained to the priesthood in St.
Paul's, Covent Garden, London, by the Bishop of Rupert's

Land, and within a month he was off to his new and far off post. He arrived at Fort Simpson, much to the astonishment of Kirkby, on Christmas Day, 1865, having made the long journey with unprecedented speed. When he reached his destination it was to discover that McDonald, who later became the first Archdeacon of the Yukon, had recovered and was able to continue his work for many years. Some years after McDonald's time it was realised that Fort Yukon was actually in Alaska, and the work was handed over to the American Church.[7] An interesting sidelight on McDonald's career has been given by a later missionary who wrote,

> There was a Church of England clergyman at Fort Yukon in the early sixties, when the Hudson [sic] Bay post flourished and fur was king, who in his journeys across country ministering to his scattered Indian flock, found gold on one of the tributaries of Birch Creek. The Reverend Robert McDonald, afterwards Archdeacon of the Yukon—and his name is still held in highest veneration by the natives—told of his discovery, and letters exist today in which it was written about, but no one at Fort Yukon cared about gold-seeking much more than Archdeacon McDonald did himself. The Hudson's Bay Company left and the post at Fort Yukon changed hands and decayed, and McDonald returned to the Mackenzie, but the story lingered and passed from mouth to mouth, and "Preacher Creek" on the map, which is certainly *not* the tributary of Birch Creek on which McDonald scooped up gold with a spoon, stands as evidence of it.[8]

The news of McDonald's recovery filled the newly-arrived Bompas with relief, although he was disappointed for himself, having set his heart on the Yukon as his particular sphere of service. He remained with Kirkby until Easter, 1866, devoting himself to learning the Indian tongue. In the summer he moved to Fort Norman where the Hudson's Bay Company had built a school and engaged a teacher to assist in ministering to the Indians.

Bompas then began the missionary journeys far and wide for which he became famous. Living in a tent and travelling on foot from post to post he covered some 1,300 miles during the next two years and preached to more than 1,500 Indians of four different tribes. In 1869 he set out to visit McDonald at Fort Yukon but on the way met a number of Eskimos who urged him to go with them down to the coast. After spending some time with them he spent the winter at the lonely Rampart House on the Peel River.

For the next few years this journeying continued but meanwhile his Diocesan, Bishop Machray, became increasingly anxious to see provision made for additional episcopal ministrations. Within ten years of his own consecration he was able to arrange for the consecration of three more bishops — John Horden for Moosonee, John McLean for Saskatchewan, and William Carpenter Bompas for Athabasca. When the news of his intended preferment reached Bompas he was horrified, and objected, "I have lived in the wilds so long that many think that I have the look of an Indian."[9] In July, 1873, he set out from his remote mission for England, firmly determined to turn the C.M.S. from any such idea, but when he reached London in the following year he was persuaded that this was no less a divine call than the one which had first taken him to the far north. He was consecrated on May 3rd, 1874, in Lambeth Parish Church by the Archbishop of Canterbury, and a few days afterwards married Charlotte Cox who was to be to him a tower of strength for the rest of his life.[10]

The Diocese of Athabasca had now come into being—a vast area stretching from close to the west side of Hudson Bay across the north to the international boundary separating Yukon and Alaska, and reaching down to include what is now known as the Peace River Block in the Diocese of Caledonia. On his return

Bishop Bompas selected Fort Simpson as his see city, and set about the organization of his huge diocese. His first synod met on September 4th, 1876 at Fort Simpson when there were present his three clergy and four or five catechists. The Bishop was not deterred, however, by small numbers or by the enormity of his task. He arranged the diocese in four great divisions as follows: first, the Tudukh Mission under the direction of Archdeacon McDonald at Fort McPherson with catechists at Rampart House and La Pierre's House; second, the Mackenzie River Mission which the Bishop supervised himself with a schoolmaster at Fort Norman and a catechist at Fort Simpson; third, the Great Slave Lake Mission, under the Reverend W. D. Reeve at Fort Rae, with a catechist at Hay River; fourth, the Athabasca Mission under the Reverend A. Shaw at Fort Chipewyan, with catechists there and at Fort Vermilion.[11]

The Bishop continued his travels during the summers, concerning which he wrote,

> To represent the length and tediousness of travel in this diocese, it may be compared to a voyage in a row-boat from the Gulf of St. Lawrence to Fort William, on Lake Superior, or a European may compare it to a voyage in a canal barge from England to Turkey. Both the length and breadth of this diocese equal the distance from London to Constantinople. . . . These extended travels prove inconsistent with domestic life, and Mrs. Bompas, being left alone in the rigourous climate, and among the sometimes chill hearts of our northern clime, has lost her health from exposure to cold and insufficient food. There is no doubt that the domestic hearth, when it can be had, will convey Christian lessons to the Indians.[12]

In the winters, with the exception of 1877-78 when he made his dramatic trip to the Pacific coast, he generally settled at one or other of the posts where there was no resident missionary.

Ten years passed after the consecration of Bishop Bompas and the work of the Church developed steadily. More clergy and lay workers were appointed. New mission stations were opened and churches built. Translations of the Bible and Prayer Book were made into a number of Indian languages. A further division of the diocese was urgent and this was effected in 1884 by the Synod of the Province of Rupert's Land. Two dioceses were created where formerly there had been one — that of the Mackenzie River stretching beyond the 60th parallel to the Arctic and westward to the Yukon, and the Diocese of Athabasca, nearer civilization, only half as large, but with great prospects.

Bompas elected to take the former diocese, retaining Fort Simpson as his headquarters but travelling far and wide as he had always done. Difficult days were ahead, however, for scarcely had the division been completed when the Bishop received word of the death of the Reverend Vincent Sim at Rampart House, one of his most able and devoted missionaries. To feed the Indians around him in a time of extreme scarcity he denied himself necessary food and so succumbed.[13] In the latter part of 1886 this famine was widespread. Game was scarce, a few moose were to be obtained, all the rabbits had died and the fish disappeared from the river. Day after day reports reached the Bishop of Indians dying of starvation. At length the situation at Fort Simpson became so serious that he left for Fort Wrigley so there might be one less mouth to feed. The situation was eased somewhat by the arrival of the supply steamer in the spring. Conditions grew very wearing for the Bishop and in the absence of Mrs. Bompas, who had returnd to England for a visit, the loneliness must have been intense. In 1890 he was living in the church at Fort Norman in extraordinarily primitive conditions, and one of his clergy wrote of him,

> An iron cup, plate, and knife, with one or two kettles, form his culinary equipment. A hole in the snow, a corner of a boat, wigwam, or log hut, provided space, 6 feet by 2 feet, for sleeping accommoda-

tion. Imagine him seated on a box in a 12-foot room, without furniture, and there cooking, teaching, studying, early and late, always at work, never at ease, never known to take a holiday.[14]

In 1891 another division took place and the Diocese of Selkirk was carved out of the existing diocese of Mackenzie River. The new diocese embraced what is now the Yukon Territory and once again Bompas chose to retain it as his see, leaving the less remote area to William Day Reeve. Bompas' first episcopal act had been to ordain Reeve to the priesthood in 1874, and on Advent Sunday, 1891, he was consecrated to succeed him as the second Bishop of Mackenzie River.

In spite of the rigours of his life, and the fact that he was a self-taught man without a university education, Bishop Bompas became a competent Biblical scholar. When Bishop Ridley visited the Bishop and his wife at Carcross in 1903 he remarked that although the living conditions left very much to be desired, "the books . . . are numerous, up to date, and as choice as any two excellent scholars could wish."[15] He went on to speak of Bishop and Mrs. Bompas, "she, accomplished far beyond the standard one meets in London drawing rooms, unless among the most cultured circles; he, a fine scholar, steeped in Hebrew and Syrian lore, as well as in the commoner studies of the clergy, live on, love on, labour on in this vast expanse little trodden but by the Indians for whom they live and will die."[16] He resigned the see at the end of October, 1905, and died less than a year later in June, 1906. He is buried in the Indian cemetery at Carcross.

Among the clergy who had come to work in the far north during this period was the Reverend Isaac O. Stringer, B.A., of Wycliffe College, Toronto, who was sent out by the Canadian Church Missionary Society. Shortly after his ordination by Bishop Reeve he made his way to Herschel Island, off the Arctic coast, and a hundred miles or so west of the mouth of the Mackenzie river. He undertook his journey "in a canvas-covered canoe, accompanied by two Indians, proceeding cautiously from island to island and point to point, but now and then having to traverse some fourteen miles of open sea."[17] There he found the Eskimos and preached to them and taught them to sing Gospel hymns. In the following year he went again, this time accompanied by Bishop Reeve and another Canadian missionary, C. E. Whittaker.

In addition to the Eskimo inhabitants Herschel Island was also occupied as an American whaling station, and the services were held in a smithy put up by the whalers with the anvil as a reading desk. The captains of the whaling fleet also contributed $600 towards the establishment of the mission. Whittaker remained there that winter but a year or so later was joined by Stringer and his bride in what Bishop Reeve described as "the most northerly inhabited spot in the British dominions, and perhaps the most inaccessible; a bleak, treeless island, ice-bound for nine months in the year, and surrounded by floating masses of it during the short summer."[18] Stringer remained with his family on Herschel Island until 1903 when he became rector of Whitehorse.

Among the other pioneer clergy was the Reverend T. H. Canham. Archdeacon Canham, as he became, was trained at the Church Missionary College, Islington, and served for a year at Portage la Prairie before going north in 1882 where he served until his retirement in 1917. In 1910 St. John's College, Winnipeg, conferred upon him the honorary degree of Doctor of Divinity in recognition of his services.

Another pioneer was the Reverend Benjamin Totty who also came from England in 1892, travelling by way of San Francisco and up the Yukon River from the Bering Sea. Beginning his work under Bishop Bompas at Forty Mile he laboured faithfully there and at Selkirk and Moosehide until his retirement in 1927.

Yet another was the Reverend John Hawksley, who began his ministry in 1891 and later became Indian Agent for the Yukon Territory.

Reference has already been made to the fact that the discovery of gold by Archdeacon McDonald and others did not at first attract much attention. In 1896, however, the excitement in California and British Columbia having died down, the Klondyke gold rush began and there followed a tremendous influx of prospectors. Bishop Bompas had laboured so long among the Indians that he found this new responsibility a severe trial, and sadly acknowledged that he had become entirely unfitted for work among the whites. He therefore accepted the services of a young layman from the Church Missionary College, Richard John Bowen, whom he later ordained, as a missionary to the miners. At the same time another young man, the Reverend Henry A. Naylor, B.A., came out from Montreal and was sent first to Forty Mile, and later to Dawson City, where he was followed by the Reverend E. P. Flewelling whom we have already met in New Westminster and Kootenay.

H. A. Cody, the biographer of Bishop Bompas, tells how, on one occasion towards the end of his life, the Bishop was asked to write a few lines in an autograph album. He at once complied and wrote the words which had first been applied to Gideon and his three hundred men, "faint yet pursuing."[19] They reflect the weariness which was stealing upon him after years of toil and hardship. In November, 1903, at the Bishop's urgent request, Stringer returned to the diocese to take up the work at Whitehorse which had been relinquished by the Reverend R. J. Bowen. The Bishop at once marked him as his successor, and two years later on November 15th, 1905, he was elected the second Bishop of Selkirk by the Electoral Committee of the Provincial Synod of Rupert's Land. The bishop-elect was consecrated in

St. John's Cathedral, Winnipeg, a month later and eagerly did Bishop Bompas look for his return. At length Bishop Stringer arrived and the aged Bishop handed on the care of the diocese which he had established.

One of Bishop Stringer's first episcopal acts was to set up a diocesan synod which met at Christ Church, Whitehorse, in September, 1907. In his primary charge the Bishop reviewed the story of missionary work in the far north and paid tribute to his predecessor as one of the heroes of the church. He passed on to speak of the episcopal endowment fund which, he suggested, might be completed as a memorial to the first bishop. It might also be necessary, he thought, to seek legal powers by which the bishop could hold property in trust for the diocese or by which the synod could be incorporated for the same purpose.

Because of the increase of population following the gold rush to the Klondyke the area contained in the Diocese of Selkirk was detached from the North West Territories and made into a separate administrative area known as the Yukon Territory. For this reason as well as to avoid confusion with better known Selkirks elsewhere it seemed well that the name of the diocese should be changed to become the Diocese of Yukon. The suggestion was endorsed in informal conferences in the diocese and the change made by unanimous vote of the Rupert's Land Provincial Synod on August 15th, 1907.[20]

The episcopate of Bishop Stringer was marked by extreme financial austerity and by the need for consolidation. Itinerant missions were developing into settled and organized parishes but at the same time the English missionary societies under whose auspices the work had been started, chiefly the C.M.S., were feeling that the time had come to withdraw their support gradually, while the newly-formed Missionary Society of the Canadian Church was only slowly able to take up the burden. In spite of a growth in numbers the white population was transitory and the work of the diocese continued to be predominantly with Indians. A problem had also arisen from the unions of miners with Indian women in remote areas where it was impossible for their children to be educated. To solve this problem Bishop Bompas opened his home to eleven Indian and half-breed children and thus organized the first residential school. Miss Mellett, who later became Mrs. R. J. Bowen, came from Ireland as the first teacher in 1893, and was, incidentally, the first unmarried white woman to enter the diocese.[21] In 1903 the school was moved to Carcross, and in 1920 St. Paul's Hostel was opened at Dawson City.

Bishop Stringer's charges to the successive synods show not only an awareness and appreciation of the mission of the Church at large but also a keen insight into matters within the diocese, and particularly those relating to the Indians and Eskimos. It is not surprising, therefore, that more and more the Church became the Indians' advocate to the Government, and representations were made seeking protection for the Indians in such matters as trapping rights, marriage laws, land tenure, medical care and education.

By 1920 the Bishop announced with obvious relief that the episcopal endowment fund had been completed. He had found the task of building it up to be a very distasteful one and it was with considerable satisfaction that he saw the sum of $50,000 placed in the hands of an investment committee in Winnipeg. Bishop Stringer remained in his northern diocese until 1931 when he was elected Metropolitan and became Archbishop of Rupert's Land.

We saw at the beginning of this chapter that the early approaches to the Yukon were generally from the east by way of the Mackenzie river. The development of the Klondyke gold field changed this, and, particularly after the construction of the

Yukon and White Pass Railway, it was found to be much easier to enter the area from the Pacific coast. In 1931 the Anglican National Commission recommended that the Diocese of Yukon should be transferred to the Ecclesiastical Province of British Columbia. The matter was discussed at length by the Diocesan synod in 1936 and it was agreed "that the Diocese of Yukon should join the Ecclesiastical Province of British Columbia, while acknowledging with gratitude the great debt that the Diocese of Yukon owes to the Province of Rupert's Land and the early missionaries who came here from that ecclesiastical Province."[22] The actual transfer, however, was delayed by the outbreak of war in 1939 and was not completed until the 1940's.

1 A. G. Morice, *History of the Catholic Church in Western Canada*, Musson Book Co., Toronto, 1910, i, p.277.
2 Eugene Stock, *History of the Church Missionary Society*, C.M.S., London, 1899, ii, p.323.
3 Morice, op. cit., i, p.282.
4 H. A. Cody, *An Apostle of the North*, Seeley, London, 1908, p.54.
5 For a sketch of his life see "Robert McDonald," by A. C. Garrioch and I. O. Stringer, *Leaders of the Canadian Church*, (second series) edited by W. Bertal Heeney, Musson Book Co., Toronto, 1920, pp.113-132.
6 Stock, op. cit., ii, p.394.
7 *Ibid.*, xii, p.325; iv, p.379.
8 Hudson Stuck, *Voyages on the Yukon and its Tributaries*, T. Werner Laurie Ltd., London, 1917, pp.85-86.
9 Fragment of an article from *Church Messenger*, Toronto, circa November, 1937, p.16.
10 Heeney, op. cit., p.267.
11 Cody, op. cit., pp.181-182.
12 *Ibid.*, pp.167 & 181.
13 Stock, op. cit., iii, p.622.
14 Cody, op. cit., p.251.
15 *Ibid.*, pp.29-294.
16 loc. cit.
17 Stock, op. cit., iii, p.624.
18 loc. cit.

19 Cody, op. cit., p.289. (Judges 8.4).
20 Proceedings, Synod of the Diocese of Yukon, September 10th, 1907, p.7.
21 *Northern Lights*, Diocese of Yukon, Vol. XXX, No. 3, August, 1941, p.3.
22 Proceedings, Synod of the Diocese of Yukon, July 12th and 13th, 1936, p.8.

# 16

## In Retrospect

So WE come to the end of our story of the Anglican Church in British Columbia and it is time to take stock of our impressions. Our initial response is surely one of admiration for the pioneer missionaries, and of respect bordering upon veneration for their fortitude in the many vicissitudes of life in a remote, new country. It is true that many of them probably went forth not knowing whither they went, scarcely suspecting the conditions which would confront them, yet to leave home for a distant and unknown land was itself no mean achievement, and their subsequent perseverance in perils of almost every kind deserves our tribute of praise and honour.

Nor were those who came men only. Nicolay had urged the sending of missionary families as being able to show an example of Christian domestic life both to pagan Indians and to dissillusioned and hardened whites. The sentiment has been echoed many times, and exemplified even more frequently in the lives of such families as the Goods, the Collisons, the Ridleys, the

Sillitoes and scores of others. That family life was not without its difficulties and hardships. Think of a mission family in some remote area with no other white family for miles, with the father of the family away on missionary journeys almost as often as he was home; of the problems connected with the education and bringing up of children. Yet the witness of Christian family life has been one of the most significant aspects of Anglican missions.

Then, too, the romance of pioneer missions must not blind us to its many trials. As we have already seen neither the white settlers nor the native Indians flocked gladly to the preaching of the Gospel as we may sometime be tempted to imagine. To many people, regardless of the colour of their skin, the preacher was suspect and only a vital Christian faith, a consuming love for people, together with the support of wife and family, enabled him to persevere with a handful of supporters in conditions primitive enough to daunt the stoutest hearts. Not even the communities were stable. Indian tribes were semi-nomadic and would disappear from time to time. White communities like Derby, Port Douglas, Fort Steele and Phoenix would wane and disappear leaving an empty church as the only memorial of a promising beginning.

The missionary who worked in such circumstances needed not only faith and perseverance, but initiative and resourcefulness. Not infrequently he had to combine the roles of priest, physician (sometimes even surgeon), teacher, judge and social worker, and it is amazing how well so many of them accomplished this. Not many of them were highly trained or brilliant scholars—many of them had been restricted to two or three years at St. Augustine's College, Canterbury or the Church Missionary College at Islington, or had even been ordained as literates after a period of reading under some bishop or priest far away from adequate libraries.

In this same connection we may call to mind the extraordinary breadth and variety of the Church's work even in the earliest days—the preaching of the word and administration of the sacraments, of course, but in addition, visitation of the whole and of the sick by land and sea; schools and reading rooms and church institutes and public lectures on a variety of subjects; marine missions, pastoral and medical; missions to Indians and Eskimos, Chinese and Japanese; and provision for the training of clergy.

This has not been carried on solely by the clergy. From the very beginnings of settlement in British Columbia the Church has received much from her devoted laymen and laywomen. This has been apparent not only in the building up of parish life but also in the work of the British Columbia Diocesan Church Society and in the establishment and activities of diocesan synods. These synods are also a reminder that the Church in British Columbia has always been conscious of her place as a part of the wider Anglican Communion. Synods with lay representation were becoming an accepted part of Anglican life outside England in the nineteenth century and their appearance here showed that the Church in British Columbia was no isolated remnant.

There were also disadvantages — the tensions of the wider Anglicanism made themselves felt in such incidents as those concerning Cridge, Duncan and Miss O'Melia, and in the two theological colleges struggling side by side for a time in Vancouver. Yet we may be thankful that in British Columbia, as in Canada generally, these tensions were never as bitter as they were elsewhere, and by the end of the period under review were showing signs of declining.

In all we may give thanks for the faithful though often unspectacular pioneers who have diligently and successfully planted the Catholic Faith as received by the Anglican Communion among the trees and mountains and islands of British Columbia.

Through their efforts, men, women and children of diverse nations and backgrounds have been brought into the Christian fellowship, have received the means of spiritual sustenance, and have then gone forth to share this faith with others.

> *They climbed the steep ascent of heaven*
> *Through peril, toil, and pain*
> *O God to us may grace be given*
> *To follow in their train.*

# Bibliography

THE SOURCES for this work may be divided roughly into five groups. First, there are the reports from the missionaries who worked in the field, supplemented by their letters and reminiscences. Some of these have been published but others are available only in manuscript form. Many of these latter are preserved in the Provincial Archives, Victoria.

A second source consists of the publications of the missionary societies in official reports and books about their work. Examples of these are the *Columbia Mission Reports,* (1859-78), Eugene Stock's *History of the Church Missionary Society,* and the more recent history of the S.P.G., *Into All Lands,* by H. P. Thompson, together with periodical publications such as *Mission Field* (S.P.G.) and the *Church Missionary Intelligencer.*

The third group consists of books and articles about particular areas written either by the missionaries themselves or by those who have wished to perpetuate their work. Such books have been mentioned frequently in the footnotes of the present volume but for general information are listed collectively at the end of this note.

Fourthly come the books describing the work of other communions and those dealing with the general history of the region. As typical of the former might be mentioned Brosnan's *Jason Lee, Prophet of the New Oregon,* Eells' *Marcus Whitman,* Morice's *History of the Catholic Church in Western Canada,* and Crosby's *Up and Down the North Pacific Coast.* Of general concern are such books as R. C. Mayne's *Four Years in British Columbia and Vancouver Island,* Richard G. Montgomery's *The White-Headed Eagle,* and Howay & Scholefield's *British Columbia.*

The fifth source is made up of miscellaneous materials, such as newspaper reports in which the *Inland Sentinel* and the *Victoria Colonist* have been particularly valuable; diocesan publications such as the *Churchman's Gazette;* synod journals and the minutes of synod executive committees, and articles from various historical magazines.

Arctander, J. W., *The Apostle of Alaska,* (William Duncan)
Fleming H. Revell, New York, 1909.
A somewhat biassed account of Duncan's work and "persecution" by the Church.

Bompas, W. C., *The Mackenzie River Diocese,*
S.P.C.K., London, 1888.
The Bishop's own account of life in the far north in the "Colonial Church Histories" series.

Brown, R. C. Lundin, *British Columbia,*
Royal Engineers Press, New Westminster, 1863.
A prize-winning essay by one of the early missionaries describing life and prospects in the Crown Colony.

Cody, H. A., *An Apostle of the North,*
Seeley & Co., London, 1908.
The life and work of Bishop Bompas by one who served as a missionary in the Yukon.

Collison, W. H., *In the Wake of the War Canoe,*
  Musson Book Co., Toronto, 1916.
  Archdeacon Collison's own account of his early work in the Queen
  Charlotte Islands and on the Skeena.
Duthie, D. Wallace, *A Bishop in the Rough,*
  Smith, Elder & Co., London, 1909.
  The life of John Sheepshanks, first rector of New Westminster and
  later Bishop of Norwich.
Gowen, H. H., *Church Work in British Columbia,*
  Longmans, Green, London, 1899.
  Early days in the diocese of New Westminster, based largely on the
  diaries of Bishop and Mrs. Sillitoe.
McCullagh, J. B., *Aiyansh, The Story of a Great Transformation,*
  C.M.S., London, 1907.
  A pamphlet describing work among the Indians in northern British
  Columbia.
Mercier, Mrs. Jerome, *Father Pat, A Hero of the Far West,*
  Minchin & Gibbs, Gloucester, 1909.
  The life of Henry Irwin with quotations from his letters and diaries.
Moeran, J. W. W., *McCullagh of Aiyansh,*
  Marshall Bros., London, 1923.
  The work of James Benjamin McCullagh among the Indians.
Janvrin, Alice J., *Snapshots of the North Pacific,*
  C.M.S., London, 1904.
  Excerpts from the writings of Bishop Ridley.
Schofield, Emily D., *Charles de Veber Schofield; late of*
  *British Columbia,*
  Victoria, 1941.
  An account of his life and reminiscences of his episcopate.
Sillitoe, Mrs. V. E., *Pioneer Days in British Columbia,* and
  *Early Days in British Columbia,*
  Two small pamphlets describing Mrs. Sillitoe's life and travels with
  her husband.
Turner, Christopher E., *A Parson Across the Rockies,*
  S.P.G., London, 1927.
  An account of the writer's work as a mission priest in the Diocese of
  Kootenay in the 1920's.

# Index